To my granddaughter
Alexandra Nicole DeCaprio
So that you will know where you come from
And who to thank

Matilda Joslyn Gage

She
Who
Holds
The
Sky

SALLY ROESCH WAGNER

Sky Carrier Press
Aberdeen, South Dakota

Cover and book design by Mary Jane Broadbent

Sky Carrier Press
P.O. Box 2135
Aberdeen, SD 57402

◦✦🙚 Acknowledgments 🙛✦◦

THANKS TO Nancy Vostad, Carol Anderson, Suzanne Pullen, Felicia Moss, Cheryl Frank, Elisabeth Dunbar and Gloria Marvin for critical assistance at different points along the way. To them is due the polish; to me, the errors. And to Mary Jane Broadbent, who made it happen.

As Gage's powerful voice has been all but silenced for so long, direct quotes are *set in a typestyle like this*. This is done with the desire to make her more familiar to you, the reader, and to further distinguish her from other sources quoted.

Sally Roesch Wagner
July 1998

Matilda Joslyn Gage at age 26 (1852)
Shown here in same dress worn at first women's rights
convention she attended.

I AM INDEBTED TO *my father for something better than a collegiate education*, Gage told the International Council of Women in 1888. *He taught me to think for myself, and not to accept the word of any man, or society, or human being, but to fully examine for myself.* The lesson took hold when Matilda, questioning religion at fifteen, came into conflict with the Baptist church fathers. True to his teaching, Hezekiah supported his daughter, assuring her, "That church are a rascally set and they will hear from me when I get home." The event marked the beginning of a long career of challenging religious authority.

Encouraged to independence of action as well, Matilda dreamed of becoming a doctor. Despite her physician father's lobbying of his professors, she couldn't break the gender barrier and gain admittance to Geneva Medical College. It would remain for a woman named Elizabeth Blackwell to do that. Married at eighteen, Matilda was the twenty-six-year-old mother of three youngsters when she answered the woman's rights call: *When I saw the reports of the first* [national, in 1850] *convention in the* **New York Tribune**, *I knew my place; and when I read the notice of a convention to be held in Syracuse, in 1852, I at once decided to publicly join the ranks of those who spoke against wrong.*

Elizabeth Cady Stanton, who lived in nearby Seneca Falls, had called the very first woman's rights convention (along with Lucretia Mott, Jane Hunt, Mary Ann McClintock and Martha Coffin Wright) in 1848. The Seneca Falls Convention was locally advertised and organized quickly, so Gage (whose son was born during this time) would not have heard about it. Although the 1848 convention held a second session in Rochester where Susan B. Anthony lived, Anthony did not attend because she thought woman's rights was a foolish ✗ issue. Her family attended, however.

Several more local conventions followed, and then yearly national conventions began in 1850. Neither Stanton, Gage nor Anthony attended the first two national conventions in Worcester, Massachusetts, but Anthony showed up for the third (1852) convention in Syracuse as an agent for Amelia Bloomer's temperance newspaper. Gage and Anthony entered the woman's rights movement together in this convention. Gage was a heart-felt supporter while Anthony's commitment to woman's rights was still lukewarm.

Gage found her voice in the 1852 convention. Unaware of protocol, *I prepared my speech and going to the convention, sat near the front and, with a palpitating heart, waited until I obtained courage to go upon the platform—probably to the interference of arrangements, for I knew nothing about the proper course for me to take.* The youngest woman on the platform, she stood before the audience of 2,000 and read her speech softly, out of nervousness and a lack of knowledge of the projection necessary to fill a large hall. *I was so sweetly welcomed by the sainted Lucretia Mott, who gave me a place, and, when I had finished speaking, referred so pleasantly to what I had said,* Gage recalled, *to her my heart turned always with truest affection.*[1]

She began her maiden speech by celebrating achievements in art, science and government despite how *trammeled women have been.* These isolated triumphs showed what all women were capable of doing. How could such tremendous potential be unleashed? Gage posed a solution to women's subordinate position that was both personal and political: Women must be educated for self-respect and economic self-reliance at the same time that the institutions that perpetuated their oppression required changing.

Having grown up in an abolitionist household, Gage well knew how vicious the backlash against justice could be. Still, it should be welcomed, as Gage explained in concluding her speech:

> *We need not expect the concessions demanded by women will be peaceably granted; there will be a long moral warfare before the citadel yields. In the meantime, let us take possession of the outposts…All great reforms are gradual. Fear not any attempt to frown down the revolution already commenced; nothing is more fertile aid of reform, than any attempt to check it; work on!*[2]

Interrupted several times by applause, her address drew a great outburst of cheering and clapping at its conclusion. Mott, who was presiding, immediately moved that the speech be published as one of their woman's rights tracts, *which I always considered a great and appreciative compliment,* Gage recalled.[3]

Shortly after, Susan B. Anthony moved that no woman should be allowed to speak whose voice could not fill the house. Paulina Wright Davis, the next scheduled speaker, vindicated Gage when she responded that she would not consent to this gag being placed on the convention, for, she told the audience "...many of her sisters had come here with full hearts, but with weak untrained voices." She would not consent "that they should have their rights thus restricted, as such a course would only perpetuate the tyranny that woman came here to destroy."[4]

Gage immediately found herself in battle with the clergy. *Soon after the close of the convention...it was criticized from the pulpit by the Rev. Mr. Ashley, of the Episcopal Church, and Rev. Mr. Sunderland...With the latter gentleman I carried on a long newspaper controversy.*[5]

Rev. Sunderland, the local Congregational minister, labeled the convention "satanic," and focused his denunciation on the sensible and modest Bloomer outfit (short dress and trousers) worn by some of the women in attendance. It was against God's will for women to adopt men's clothing, Rev. Sunderland warned his congregation, quoting Deuteronomy 22:5: "The woman shall not wear that which pertaineth unto a man, neither shall a man put on a woman's garment: for all that do so are abomination unto the Lord thy God."

When his sermon was printed in a Syracuse paper, someone identified simply as "M" (Gage's identity remained unknown to the paper's readers) challenged the minister. *He being one of the priesthood ignores the Bible himself, since he does not minister in a robe whose hem is trimmed with bells of gold, neither does he wear a bonnet of fine linen,* "M" chastised. Rev. Sunderland should recognize that men were greater sinners than Bloomer-wearers for *had not men, in their attempts to acquire feminine resemblance, progressed past both nature's law and the law of Moses (Leviticus 21:5)*[6] *forbidding men to shave or 'mar the corner of their beards,'* there would be no confusion of sexual identity. The ecclesiastical duel continued for several weeks in the local paper, much to the delight of Syracuse readers, especially when they discovered that the person who was running biblical circles around the minister was a woman! Gage challenged Rev. Sunderland's orthodox interpretation of the Scriptures, and teased him with an "Adam was a rough draft" joke:

> *With regard to Eve and the authority for her being bound to consult her husband in the relation established by the creation of the first pair, some persons might think the order of creation would imply just the contrary; for as we trace the progress of creation step by step, we perceive that the inferior were first made and each successive thing created, exceeded in rank the preceding one.*[7]

Gage had the last word thirty-six years later. Reminiscing about the Sunderland debates during her speech at the 1888 International Council of Women, Gage pondered, *it is not religion that has opposed woman suffrage, because true religion believes in undoing the heavy burdens and letting the oppressed go free. But from the church and from theology this reform has met opposition at every step.*[8] Her ideas about the church did not come late in life. By the age of 26, Gage was a seasoned veteran at challenging organized religion.

The Beginning of Organization

A S THE WOMAN'S MOVEMENT spread quickly in the 1850s, Gage, Stanton and Anthony each developed her own political style. Gage continued her abolition activities, begun when she'd circulated anti-slavery petitions in childhood. In 1850, as a twenty-four-year-old wife and mother living near Syracuse in the village of Manlius, New York, Gage signed a petition stating that she would face a six-month prison term and a $2,000 fine rather than obey the noxious Fugitive Slave law. The Gage family moved to Fayetteville in 1854 and their home was (according to family tradition) a station on the Underground Railroad, as had been the home of her parents. Gage lived in this house, which still stands on the corner of Walnut and East Genessee, for the rest of her life.

The Gage home in Fayetteville, NY (circa 1900)

Matilda Joslyn Gage at age 35 (1861)

"It may be said of her—she is an unpublished author," Helen Leslie Gage wrote about her mother many years later. "From childhood she has written stories, verses, essays, lectures, etc., some of which have been destroyed, others still lie about the house." The oldest child Helen had a brother, Thomas Clarkson (named for the famous English abolitionist), and a younger sister Julia by the 1850s and had lost an infant brother. Another sister, Maud, would come along in the next decade. With little ones at home, Gage tried her hand at political fiction during the heyday of women authors in the 1850s, publishing serialized short stories and poetry along with letters to the editor on women's wages and other issues.

Despite her child-raising responsibilities, Gage appeared at the next two national conventions that became yearly events during the 1850s (New York City in 1853, Philadelphia in 1854) and began an active involvement in state activities as well. Anthony (who rapidly converted to woman's rights after the Syracuse convention) became an organizer, attending most state and national conventions. Gage came to her rescue in 1854, organizing a last-minute convention in Saratoga Springs. The previous year, Gage had served as a vice president at a state convention and worked on the Industrial Committee as well.

Stanton, on the other hand, hated conventions, avoiding every one she could. Her (eventually) seven children gave her ample excuse. Nor was she fond of door-to-door petition work or of seeing to the organizational details. Stanton's work was primarily done with a pen during this time, as she wrote a steady stream of convention addresses, newspaper articles and columns for the *Lily*, the Seneca Falls temperance paper edited by Amelia Bloomer.

Childless and able to support herself during this decade as an anti-slavery (and briefly, woman's rights) lecturer, Anthony possessed the time, money and mobility to travel about taking care of the business of the movement and attending conventions. She didn't trust her political instincts much in the beginning, preferring to trust in the eagerly given advice of Stanton on matters of strategy and theory. The characteristic that would limit her activities throughout Anthony's life emerged during this time. By her own repeated admission, she couldn't write a word. This moment in the 1850s stands frozen in time as historians have placed a pen permanently in Stanton's hand as she forges one speech after another for Anthony to go off and deliver. In truth, this writer/speaker relationship between Stanton and Anthony began to change before the Civil War as Stanton's children grew and she began delivering her own speeches.

By the Civil War, Stanton was living in New York City where she and Anthony organized the Women's Loyal National League. While Lincoln insisted that the war was being fought only to preserve the Union and had nothing to do with slavery, the League gathered pledges from over 300,000 Northern citizens vowing they would only support the war effort if its goal was to end slavery.

Gage joined the League and gathered signatures. In 1862, when asked to present a flag to the Fayetteville regiment of New York volunteers (according to the local paper "the village was out en masse,") Gage made no bones about the war's cause before the large crowd. The war between the North and the South, she announced, *is a war of principles. On the one hand, Liberty and the Union, and the poor man's rights forever; and on the other, slavery and the aristocratic disunion of a few over both the black man and the poor white man.*

While a number of women also made flag-presentation speeches, Gage's uniquely called upon the soldiers to take responsibility for the conditions under which they would fight: to end slavery.

There can be no permanent peace, Gage insisted, *until the cause of the war is destroyed. And what caused the war? Slavery! And nothing else. That is the corner stone and keystone of the whole. The cries of downtrodden millions arising to the throne of God. Let each one of you feel the fate of the world to be upon your shoulders, and fight for yourselves, and us, and the future.*

Gage went further: *Let Liberty be your watchword and your war cry alike. Unless liberty is attained—the broadest, the deepest, the highest liberty for **all**—not for one set alone, one clique alone, but for man and woman, black and white, Irish, Germans, Americans and Negroes, there can be no permanent peace.*[9] Defined in these startlingly broad terms, there are those who would argue that the

Civil War is still not over.

Although a member, Gage was not centrally involved after 1865 (as were Stanton and Anthony) in the Equal Rights Association which worked for suffrage for both women and African American men after the war. When the white men in that organization determined that it should put all its efforts toward gaining the vote for African American men and proceeded to cut off funds for woman suffrage campaigns, Gage joined with Anthony, Stanton and other radical suffragists to form the National Woman Suffrage Association (NWSA) in 1869. At the same time, the women who were willing to temporarily put aside the struggle for their rights in favor of "the Negro's hour" formed the American Woman Suffrage Association (AWSA), joined by some men like Lucy Stone's husband, Henry Blackwell.

Stanton and Parker Pillsbury (one of the three men who supported the NWSA's formation) edited a paper called the *Revolution* for two years. The paper was published by Anthony and Gage was one of the paper's principal contributors.

The Suffrage Decade

THE DECADE in which the movement can correctly be called a "suffrage" one is during the 1870s, when woman's absence from the polls emerged as the most obvious right she was denied.

Having created a political presence for themselves during the Civil War, loyal women of the North assumed that they would be formally acknowledged as players in the postwar period. Gage, Stanton and Anthony, editors of the *History of Woman Suffrage*, wrote: "If moral power has any value in the balance with physical force, surely the women of this republic, by their self-sacrifice and patriotism, their courage 'mid danger, their endurance 'mid suffering, have rightly earned a voice in the laws they were compelled to obey, in the Government they are taxed to support..."[10]

NATIONAL WOMAN SUFFRAGE ASSOCIATION.

President, ELIZABETH CADY STANTON, Tenafly, N. J.
First Vice President, LUCRETIA MOTT, Philadelphia, Pa.
Chairman Executive Committee. MATILDA JOSLYN GAGE. Fayetteville, N. Y.
Corresponding Secretary, SUSAN B. ANTHONY, Rochester, N. Y.

1776. CENTENNIAL QUESTIONS. 1876.

Why should women, more than men, be governed without their consent?
Why should women, more than men, be taxed without representation?
Why should women, more than men, be tried without a jury of their peers?
By what right do men declare themselves invested with power to legislate for women in all cases whatsoever?

Should Women more than Men be governed without their own consent?

WOMEN CITIZENS!
A Mass Meeting in the interest of all Women

WHO WANT TO VOTE
WILL BE HELD AT

FARWELL HALL, 148 MADISON STREET,
TUESDAY, JUNE 1st, 1880,
AT 10 A. M., 2:30 AND 8 P. M.
UNDER AUSPICES OF THE

NATIONAL WOMAN SUFFRAGE ASSOCIATION.

— THE CONVENTION WILL BE ADDRESSED BY

Susan B. Anthony, Matilda Joslyn Gage, Belva A. Lockwood, Sara Andrews Spencer, Lill
Devereaux Blake, Phœbe W. Couzins, Elizabeth L. Saxon, Elizabeth Boynton Harbert,
E. Haggart, and representative Men and Women from all sections of the United St

THE JNO. B. JEFFERY PRINTING HOUSE, CHICAGO.

TOP: *NWSA envelope (1876)*
ABOVE: *NWSA handbill (1880)*
LEFT: *Proceedings of the founding convention, Woman's National Liberal Union (1890)*

Woman's National Liberal Union

CONVENTION FOR ORGANIZATION
—— HELD ——

February 24-25, 1890,

WILLARD'S HALL.   -   -   -   WASHINGTON, D. C.

ORGANIZATION AND PLAN OF WORK.

SEC. 1. The management of the business affairs and plans of the Woman's National Liberal Union shall be vested in an Executive Council consisting of nine persons.

SEC. 2. The following officers shall be elected from among and by the Executive Council: A President, a Vice-President, a Secretary and a Treasurer, to hold office for one year or until their successors are elected.

SEC. 3. The Executive Council shall have the power to fill all vacancies and to create such additional offices as may be deemed necessary to fully carry out the objects of the Union.

OFFICERS.

MATILDA JOSLYN GAGE, President, Fayetteville, N. Y.
JOSEPHINE CABLES ALDRICH, Vice-President, Aldrich, Ala.
MARY EMILY RATES COUES, Cor. Secretary, 1736 N St., Washington, D. C.
W. F. ALDRICH, Treasurer, Aldrich, Ala.
MRS. MECCA HOFFMAN, Enterprize, Kan.
SUSAN H. WIXON, Fall River, Mass.
MARIETTA M. BONES, Webster, South Dakota.
ELIZA ARCHARD CONNOR, 34 Vesey St., New York.
CLARA S. FOLTZ, San Diego, Cal.

PROVISIONAL COMMITTEE.

Consisting of one person in each State and Territory, to be appointed by the Executive Council and known as State Managers. Work planned by the Executive Council.

Instead, African American and white women watched as African American men alone were granted suffrage in 1870 with the Fifteenth Amendment, while the Fourteenth Amendment, adopted in 1868, protected their voting rights. The Fourteenth Amendment appeared to be a substantial setback for women at the time of its passage. The federal government would protect the rights of citizens if threatened by the actions of states, the Amendment promised, warning that "no state shall make or enforce any law which shall abridge the privileges or immunities of citizens of the United States." As worded, however, citizens were defined as men three times in the document. Introducing the word "male" into the constitution for the first time, the Amendment threw into question whether women were even citizens.

The Fourteenth Amendment was a double-edged sword. While it said citizens were male, it also defined the role of the federal government as protector of citizens whose rights were being violated by the states. Gage used the contradiction to make a compelling argument, which formed the theoretical foundation for the NWSA's suffrage work in the 1870s. Women's rights were being denied by the states, Gage maintained in her *Woman's Rights Catechism*, and the federal government had the legal responsibility to protect them. Her logic was relentless:

Q: FROM WHENCE DO GOVERNMENTS DERIVE THEIR JUST POWERS?
A: ...From the consent of the governed. —Declaration of Independence.

Q: ARE RIGHTS GRANTED PEOPLE BY GOVERNMENTS OR THROUGH CONSTITUTIONS?
A: No. Rights existed before governments are founded or constitutions created.

Q: OF WHAT USE THEN ARE GOVERNMENTS AND INSTITUTIONS?
A: To protect people in the exercise and enjoyment of their natural and fundamental rights, which existed before governments or constitutions were made. —Declaration of Independence and Constitution.

Q: WHAT IS A CITIZEN?
A: In the United States, a citizen is a person, native or naturalized, who has the privilege of exercising the elective franchise. —Webster

Q: WHAT PERSONS ARE CITIZENS OF THE UNITED STATES?
A: All persons born or naturalized in the United States, and subject to the jurisdiction thereof, are citizens of the United States, and of the State wherein they reside.
—14th Amendment

Q: WHAT RIGHT HAS A CITIZEN OF THE UNITED STATES?
A: The right to vote...

Q: WHAT LAW OF THE UNITED STATES ESPECIALLY ENFORCES THE RECOGNITION OF THE POLITICAL RIGHTS OF ITS CITIZENS?
A: A law passed by the 42d Congress of the United States and signed by the President (April 19, 1871), which declares that "any person, who under color of any law, statute, ordinance, regulation, custom or usage of any State, shall subject, or cause to be subjected, any person within the jurisdiction of the United States, to the deprivation of any rights, privileges, or immunities secured by the Constitution of the United States, shall, any law to the contrary notwithstanding, be liable to the penalty required in any action at law or equity...

Q: ARE THOSE PERSONS WHO, UNDER COLOR OF LAW, FORBID WOMAN THE BALLOT, LAW-KEEPERS OR LAW-BREAKERS?
A: They are law-breakers, acting in defiance to both national and state law, in thus refusing to women citizens the exercise of a right secured to them by the Constitution of the United States; and they render themselves liable to prosecution thereby.[11]

While it could not "grant" women the right to vote (since that right was fundamental to every citizen in a democracy), the federal government had a responsibility to protect women's inherent right of suffrage with a constitutional amendment, Gage reasoned, just as it had done for African American men with the Fifteenth Amendment. In the meantime, the NWSA women determined to exercise their right of citizenship. The *Woman's Rights Catechism* provided the theoretical framework for a brilliant strategy designed to hold the government accountable to its principles through a campaign of non-violent civil disobedience.

It was against the law for women to vote. But women voted, (or tried to) by the hundreds, all across the country, claiming they had the right as tax-paying citizens of the republic. They were not the law-breakers, Gage made clear; the states carried that distinction. If arrested for voting, women would use the argument in their defense. If not allowed to vote, they would use it in bringing suit against the voter registrars who denied them their exercise of citizenship.

The arrest and trial of Susan B. Anthony for the crime of voting captured the nation's attention in 1872, a presidential election year. The countless other women who had gone to the polls had not been arrested and Gage—alone among the suffragists—recognized that the government was making a test case of the country's best-known suffragist in an attempt to stop their voting campaign.[12]

Anthony and Gage treated it as a political trial, speaking throughout Monroe County (where Anthony had been arrested) and educating potential jurors on the issue. When the district attorney got a change of venue to Ontario County, Anthony made twenty-one speeches in the twenty-two days before the trial began, while Gage spoke in sixteen additional townships.

As with her flag-presentation speech the decade before, Gage helped the participants understand the part they were playing in history. This was a special gift of Gage, to recognize the historic importance of the moment and empower people with the knowledge that they, and not some inevitable and predestined force of history, would bring in the future by their actions at that moment.

To you, men of Ontario County, has come an important hour. The fates have brought about that you, of all the men in this great land, have the responsibility of this trial. To you, freedom has come looking for fuller acknowledgment, for a wider area in which to work and grow. Your decision will not be for Susan B. Anthony alone; it will be for yourselves and for your children's children to the latest generation...No more momentous hour has arisen in the interest of freedom, for the underlying principles of the republic, its warp and woof alike, is the exact and permanent political equality of every citizen of the nation, whether that citizen is native born or naturalized, white or black, man or woman. And may God help you.[13]

Judge Hunt, described by Gage as *a small-brained, pale-faced, prim-looking man,* was nervous on the day of the trial, knowing that most potential jurors in the county had heard about the significance of the case and the issues it raised from Gage and Anthony's speaking tour and the newspaper accounts of their talks. But the judge was ready. Gage wryly commented, *this was the first criminal case he had been called on to try since his appointment, and with remarkable forethought, he had penned his decision before hearing it.* Violating Anthony's constitutional right to a jury trial, the judge did not allow the jury to decide the case, nor did he consult them or allow them to indicate their opinion in any way. Judge Hunt found Susan B. Anthony guilty of voting (an act expressly forbidden to women under New York law) and fined her one hundred dollars plus the costs of the prosecution. She refused to pay.

While the government arrested Anthony for its test case, the National Woman Suffrage Association created their own test case. NWSA officer Virginia Minor sued Reese Happersett, a St. Louis registrar who refused to let her vote, for $10,000. (Actually, her husband filed the case on her behalf; as a married woman, she could neither sue nor be sued under Missouri law.) The Minors carried her case all the way to the United States Supreme Court. The 1874 decision was unanimous. Women did not have the right to vote protected in the United States. It was also permanent, the nine Supreme Court justices agreeing: "If the courts can consider any question settled, this is one." In the court's decision, Chief Justice Morrison R. Waite declared that suffrage was not coexistent with citizenship, that states had the absolute right to grant or deny suffrage. Further, in the court's opinion: "The Constitution of the United States does not confer the right of suffrage upon any one."[14]

Ably reviewing the case in a subsequent NWSA convention, Gage proved that the United States government had in fact created eight different groups of voters, including those men who had previously been slaves. Confederate leaders, who had lost the vote as traitors, were given the vote back again by federal law after they were granted amnesty.

One law journal thought the ruling was as absurd as it was dangerous, stating: "If, then, the United States has no voters in the States, [which was the foundation of the Minor decision] it can properly have nothing to do with the subject of elections." Ultimately, the federal government "will be completely at the mercy" of the states, the *Central Law Journal* worried.[15]

This may have been the point. The Southern states were once again denying citizenship rights to African American men, while the federal government stood by and watched it happen. In failing to protect citizen's rights against the states, the government violated the Fourteenth Amendment. If it consciously broke the law by refusing to stop states from denying voting rights to Black men, was the federal government likely to protect the voting rights of all women? The prophetic words of Gage's flag-presentation speech rang true. *Unless liberty is attained—the broadest, the deepest, the highest liberty for all—there can be no permanent peace.* The struggle for the rights of African American men and all women were linked.

Out of the Supreme Court defeat, Matilda Joslyn Gage came up with a unique strategy. As the Republican leadership abandoned Radical Reconstruction in the South by withdrawing Union troops in 1877 and averting their eyes from the Ku Klux Klan violence that resulted, they also began granting amnesty to former Confederate leaders and allowing them to vote again. The Amnesty Act of 1872 was followed by individual acts of Congress removing the legal and political disabilities of almost 5,000 men. If Congress could refranchise traitors, could it not franchise loyal women?

Another group of men that Gage demonstrated had been enfranchised by the United States and not by individual states were those convicted of breaking a civil law. Though their right of suffrage had been taken away, 2,500 convicted criminals within the previous five years had successfully petitioned Congress to regain that right. If Congress could give felons the right to vote, why couldn't they do it for law-abiding women? Gage drew up a "Petition for Relief from Political Disabilities," similar to the ones that gave Confederate soldiers and felons the right to vote again. Gage's congressional representative accordingly introduced the bill in 1877 to declare Matilda Joslyn Gage "a citizen of the United States, clothed with all the political rights and powers of citizenship, namely: the right to vote and hold office to the same extent and in the same degree that male citizens enjoy these rights."

The NWSA as an organization picked up the tactic, and one paper correctly predicted that these relief petitions would "drop in on Congress like hailstones." Within a few years, hundreds of women from around the country had petitioned the government to grant them the same right of suffrage it gave to convicted felons and traitors. While the bills (not surprisingly) did not pass, they did gain press notice and brought the subject of woman suffrage before Congress, paving the way for the introduction (in 1878) of the Federal Suffrage Amendment.[16]

Taking the long view, Gage recognized the significance of their voting campaign:

> *Never have trials taken place which meant so greatly of good or evil to all womankind as those of woman under the Fourteenth Amendment, and although every decision of state, or circuit, or Supreme Court has been against them…yet woman has not been vanquished. There are defeats which mean more than victories in their remote results, and the decisions against woman in all these trials are of that character. Not a woman who before had striven for suffrage felt disheartened. Their courage rose with every opposing argument or decision, while thousands and tens of thousands whose thoughts had not been turned to this battle*

for the rights of their sex, now felt the indignity heaped upon them through false interpretations of law by those in power, joined hands and worked with the heretofore despised reformer.[17]

The next stage of the civil disobedience campaign developed out of the contradiction exposed by the voting stage. *Oh, wise men,* Gage chided, *can you tell why he means she, when taxes are to be assessed, and does not mean she, when taxes are to be voted upon…If you did not allow the votes of those ten women who offered them at your charter election, because they were women, pray be consistent, and do not tax them for the same reason.* The government's inconsistency, she contended, meant that *the money used to prosecute Miss Anthony was illegally collected. The whole question of a woman's demand for a vote along with taxation is a simple question of justice,* Gage claimed.[18]

While individual women had refused to pay their taxes for years, an organized campaign of tax resistance began on December 16, 1873—the Centennial of the Boston Tea Party. The New York Woman Suffrage Association called a mass meeting for that day, inviting "the tax paying women of New York…to protest against the tyranny of taxation without representation."

Gage reminded the audience that the original tax protesters had been the revolutionary mothers when *the women of New England… united themselves into a league, and bound themselves to use no more tea in their families until the tax upon it was repealed…These public protests against taxation were…the real origin of the famous Tea Party in Boston Harbor, which did not take place until three years after the public protest of the women.*

The women of today are the direct posterity of the women of the Revolution, Gage concluded, *and as our foremothers protested against taxation without representation, so do we, their descendants, protest against being taxed without being represented.*[19]

Gage, Anthony and Lillie Devereux Blake subsequently addressed the Judiciary Committee of the New York legislature, requesting a bill exempting all women from the payment of taxes until given the vote, as dozens of women withheld their taxes from the government in protest.

Declaration of Rights of Women: 1876

WHEN THE NATION prepared to celebrate the centennial, the National Woman Suffrage Association declared that: "The women of the United States, denied for one hundred years the only means of self-government—the ballot—are political slaves, with greater cause for discontent, rebellion and revolution, than the men of 1776." Like Abigail Adams, "We believe that the passion for liberty cannot be strong in the breasts of those who are accustomed to deprive their fellow-creatures of liberty." Just as Abigail Adams predicted, "'We are determined to foment a rebellion, and will not hold ourselves bound by laws in which we have no voice or representation,'" the suffragists warned.

For all the shame of those years they would leave one bright remembrance for the women of the next Centennial, in taking a grander step towards freedom than ever before, Gage vowed. Her plan was to write a *Declaration of Rights of Women: If our present declaration cannot be so interpreted as to cover the rights of women; we must issue one that will,* she promised.

The Spring of 1876 was a busy time for Gage, as she wrote a friend, *I am almost dead with overwork, having **been** the National Woman Suffrage Association for the last six months, doing the duty of President, Secretary, Chair of the Executive Committee and partly of Treasurer.*[20] Gage rented headquarters in Philadelphia and the radical suffragists decided to **demand justice for the women of this land** by presenting a *Woman's Declaration of Rights* at the official ceremonies on July 4. Gage and Stanton penned the document and then asked for permission to present it. They were denied on the grounds that, if granted, "it would be the event of the day—the topic of discussion to the exclusion of all others."

Lucretia Mott and Elizabeth Cady Stanton decided that they would not even sit on the platform after all the rebuffs the women had received. But Matilda Joslyn Gage, Susan B. Anthony, Sara Andrews Spencer, Phebe Couzins and Lillie Devereux Blake, who were "braver and more determined," according to Stanton, made a different decision. They decided to go ahead with their plan, risking arrest in order to *place on record for the daughters of 1976, the fact that their mothers of 1876 had thus asserted their equality of rights, and thus impeached the government of today for its injustice towards women,* Gage explained.

On July 4, 1876, the five women took their seats in the press section facing a crowd of 150,000 in Independence Square. When a descendant of one of the original signers finished reading the Declaration of Independence, they made their move. They had only a few seconds to reach the speaker's platform before the guards surrounding it would stop them. Anthony went first, followed by Gage who held the three-foot scroll containing the *Declaration.* They moved rapidly and as they approached the stand, the foreign guests, military officers and guards—taken by surprise—all made way. Gage passed their document to Anthony who placed it in the hand of a startled Vice President Ferry saying "we present this Declaration of Rights of the women citizens of the United States." With his silent acceptance, the Declaration became an official part of the day's proceedings. Their historic deed accomplished, the five women turned and quickly walked out, scattering printed copies of the *Declaration* as they went.

Making their way through the crowd to the musician's platform in front of Independence Hall, Gage held an umbrella over Anthony to protect her friend from the hot noonday sun while Anthony publicly read for the first time, to a cheering crowd, the *Woman's Declaration of Rights and Articles of Impeachment against the Government of the United States.*

In the grand celebration held afterwards at the Unitarian church, where each of the women addressed a different topic in the *Declaration,* Gage explained that *habeas corpus* was suspended in the case of married women who, as a result, had no protection against imprisonment by their husbands. This was no small matter, given the widespread practice of wife battering, and the frequency of femicide (murder of wives), she noted.

The *Declaration* concluded with these words: "And now, at the close of a hundred years…We ask of our rulers, at this hour, no special favors, no special privileges, no special legislation. We ask justice, we ask equality, we ask that all the civil and political rights that belong to citizens of the United States be guaranteed to us and our daughters forever." Hundreds of women signed the *Declaration*, including ninety-four African American women from the District of Columbia.[21]

History of Women Suffrage

GAGE CLOSED THE National Woman Suffrage Association headquarters in Philadelphia in November and went to join Anthony at Stanton's home in Tenafly, New Jersey, where the three leaders began to work on a history of their movement. The concept of the *History of Woman Suffrage* had taken form in conversations during the summer in their suffrage head-quarters. Anthony initially approached Gage to write it by herself, believing that with her knowledge and writing talent, Gage could toss it off in two months. More realistically, Gage thought the three women could do it in three to five years. Had they known it would take ten years, and result in three volumes of almost 1,000 pages each, they might never have begun. The preliminary job of sorting and arranging papers covering thirty years of activity seemed overwhelming in itself.[22]

Drawing primarily on Anthony and Gage's accumulated boxes of newspaper clippings, letters and pamphlets ("Mrs. Gage has a wonderful file of facts and data," Anthony marveled[23]), the women soon realized they would need to enlist assistance. Gage's commit-ment to drawing more women into the project was philosophical as well as practical. *In order to get a full and true account,* the per-ceptions and memories of many would be required to reconstruct events, she believed.[24]

The form of the *History* took shape as they worked. Veteran reform activists from the various states were asked to write up "a general résumé of what has been done, by whom and when." Prominent workers were asked to write up their reminiscences or provide information for short biographical sketches.

The responsibilities emerged and were divided: writing request letters, rewriting the copy received, filling in the gaps and compiling the parts of the story that did not fall into assigned categories. Gage described their respective duties: *Susan B. Anthony does not write, you know—she says so, again and again and it is true. Her forte is letters—nothing otherwise, but she is a good suggestor, critic, etc., looks over letters, reads proof, attends to the publishers, etc., is general factotum while Mrs. Stanton and myself do the writing.*[25]

The three editors drew up a contract, delineating what they expected from each other. Gage and Stanton would "write, collect, select and arrange the material for said history" while Anthony, "as her part of the work, and as an equivalent for the work done" by Stanton and Gage, would "secure the publication of said work by and through some competent publishing house." The net profits would be divided equally among the three.[26]

Political differences emerged among the editors, with Anthony generally being outvoted by Stanton and Gage. She objected to the "absurd" statement Stanton penned in the Preface for Volume III that the legislature is the primary source of governmental power. Gage sided with Stanton, and the sentence remained as written. Anthony was opposed to printing Gage's carefully reasoned and thoroughly documented account of the primary role of the church in maintaining the oppression of women. Anthony consistently believed the movement should focus on the single issue of suffrage, and opposed ruffling the feathers of conservative Christian women and the clergy. Stanton and Gage believed that the ideological underpinnings of the denial of woman's rights could be traced to church law, and once again overruled their coadjutor. *Woman, Church and State* appeared at the conclusion of Volume I, a forty-six-page preliminary study for Gage's major work of the same name published in 1893.[27]

The theoretical differences that emerged among the three editors were not as serious as disagreements over money and credit, however. Although having pledged in their contract to supply her coeditors with monthly financial statements, Anthony provided only one in nine and a half years, and that a most unsatisfactory one, Gage believed. She and Stanton suspected that Anthony was charging expenses from suffrage campaigns and conventions to the *History*. Gage badly needed any profits that might come from the *History* since she and her invalid husband were suffering from the economic panic that had seized the country. In 1883, when Stanton and Anthony went off to vacation in Europe, Gage was talking privately of mortgaging her house to meet living expenses. Anthony wanted to give away books to notable people and libraries while Stanton and Gage wanted to see some profit from their years of work. The financial conflict appears to have been imperfectly resolved when Anthony bought out the shares Gage and Stanton held in the *History*.[28]

The problem of credit for the work was never resolved and remains unresolved to this day. Gage has never received proper acknowledgement of her co-authorship of the *History*. As early as 1880 a *New York Herald* reporter called upon Anthony and Stanton in Tenafly, and the women claimed the *History* as their product, never mentioning Gage. At another time, Gage was presiding at the annual National Woman Suffrage Association convention when Anthony got up and mentioned the *History* that "she and Mrs. Stanton had prepared," totally ignoring Gage who was there in the Chair. *I feel such things and they wrong me,* Gage confided to a friend. *It is really* **Hamlet** *with Hamlet left out.*[29]

Although it is impossible to determine who exactly did what writing and rewriting on the *History*, it appears from known authorship that the amount of Gage's writing at least equaled that of Stanton's. And had she written only one line it would have exceeded the writing of Anthony, who time and again insisted, "It is out of the question for me to write a line...whenever I take a pen in hand I always seem to be mounted on stilts." Gage also appears to have put as much time into the *History* as did her coeditors, and in some cases, more.[30]

Anthony, who outlived the other two women, continued in her single-minded quest for the vote. She picked a journalist, Ida Husted Harper, to write her biography. When they finished that project,

The four children of Matilda Joslyn Gage (circa 1876)
CLOCKWISE FROM TOP:
Thomas Clarkson (named for the noted English abolitionist),
Maud, Helen Leslie, Julia Louise

Harper and Anthony edited a fourth volume of the *History*. The book picked up where the third volume had left off in 1883 and carried the history of woman rights work to 1900. Harper, who became the official historian of the National American Woman Suffrage Association, finished the *History* in two more volumes, which ended the story with the passage of the woman suffrage amendment to the Constitution in 1920. These six volumes stand, as Stanton correctly predicted, as the major source for anyone wishing to study the "most momentous reform that has yet been launched on the world—the first organized protest against the injustice which has brooded over the character and destiny of one-half the human race."[31]

Harper and Anthony wrote Gage out of the *History* in their fourth volume, published after Gage's death. They describe Anthony as the major worker on the first three volumes, Stanton the "matchless writer" and Gage is cast as someone whom "on many occasions they called to their aid for historical facts."[32]

The period of producing the *History* (1876-1886) may have been the busiest ten years in Gage's life, with family responsibilities and work. Her four children all married within a few years (her son in Dakota Territory) and she gave all three of her daughters formal home weddings. Among the gifts she gave Julia and her husband Frank was a set of the *History* with the inscription: *That they allow the principles of justice to rule their lives irrespective of race, color, condition or sex, is the desire of Mother.*[33]

Her husband Henry took sick and Matilda managed his business affairs while she nursed him through his final illness. Four grandchildren were born during this time.

Suffrage work took another form after the protest period of the early 1870s and Gage continued in the forefront of action. When Senator Sargent from California (whose wife, Ellen Clark, was the treasurer of the NWSA) introduced a woman suffrage amendment in 1878, the organization gathered 30,000 names within four months on petitions asking Congress to approve the amendment. Gage was included on the "Workers Honor Roll" for the large number of signatures she had gathered. Neither Stanton nor Anthony's names were on the Roll.[34]

The women's rights movement had proven, through its relentless activism and high visibility, that it must be taken seriously as a political force, and President Hayes agreed to meet with NWSA representatives during their 1879 convention in Washington. Matilda Joslyn Gage, as Chair of the Presidential Committee, read an address to President Hayes, *which evidently surprised him by its brevity and directness* and impressed the reporters covering the story, as well.

Gage worked hard in 1880 to gain New York women the right to vote and run for office in school elections. The New York Woman Suffrage Association used an interesting tactic to achieve their goal. Governor Robinson vetoed a bill giving women the right to serve on school boards when it initially passed the legislature. When he ran for re-election, the New York suffragists resolved to defeat him. They were successful, and the new Governor promptly asked the legislature to pass the bill again for his signature. They did so. Governor Cornell immediately signed the new bill. Gage interpreted their victory as a call for vigorous action:

> *When men begin to fear the power of women, their voice and their influence, then we shall secure justice, but not before. When we demonstrate our ability to kill off, or seriously injure a candidate, or hurt a party, then we shall receive "respectful consideration."...We must be recognized as aggressive.*

Gage's extensive organizing work with the women in her hometown paid off at this time. In the next school election, Fayetteville women turned out in droves and elected an all-women slate of officers, including Gage's oldest daughter Helen, who was elected clerk.[35]

Matilda Joslyn Gage (circa 1886)

The Anti's

A T THE SAME TIME, anti-suffrage women began petitioning and speaking before Congress in opposition to women voting. Suffrage would move women out of their God-given sphere, these conservative women feared. Seeing the contradiction inherent in their public action on behalf of keeping women in the home, Gage, as Chair of the Committee on Arrangements, invited Mrs. Admiral Dahlgren and her anti-suffrage friends to attend the NWSA convention and *let us know your reason for the faith that is within you.* Since *you have publicly expressed your opposition to woman's enfranchisement, not only through the papers, but also by a petition against it to Congress, we feel sure you will gladly accept our invitation,* Gage insisted. Mrs. Dahlgren responded that by even asking them to debate, Gage had entirely ignored the principle that they sought to defend "the preservation of female modesty. Our men must be brave and our women modest, if this country may hope to fulfill her true mission for humanity," Mrs. Dahlgren sniffed, declining to debate.[36]

After thirty years of meeting, writing, speaking, petitioning and protesting (unsuccessfully) for the protection of a right that was already theirs, the handwriting was on the wall. The problem was far deeper than a superficial political one. Slavery was not a metaphor for the condition of women; it *was* the condition of women. And it was not just the right, it was the responsibility of the slave to revolt.

Gage wrote to her local paper in 1878, outraged that *half a dozen young girls were arrested for streetwalking in Fayetteville,* while *their male companions in vice were not arrested, for, under the law of the State of New York, though street-walking is held to be a crime in woman, it is no offence in a man.* Two of the girls were only fifteen; the men who were "village respectables" went free and unnamed in court. The young women could not sue and had no redress. This was simply one instance of the injustice towards women, Gage maintained, and women should not rest until they had achieved *the exact and permanent civil, religious and political equality of man and woman.*

Protest, petition, write, speak, use all your powers and free yourselves and your daughters from the slavery you are under, for women are neither more nor less than SLAVES. If you do not thus work, you are criminals in the sight of your Maker. If you do not thus protest, you are unfit for freedom; and you and your daughters must suffer until, from the depths of your degradation, you are made to feel you have souls within you which are your own—until you grow to learn that your accountability is to your Creator and not to man.

Political Campaigns, Protests and Writing Them Up

WHILE SHE ENVISIONED nothing short of a revolution, Gage continued to hope, along with the NWSA, that change could come from the existing political system. *Our political predilections…are generally Republican,* Gage wrote the Secretary of the National Republican Committee, offering the NWSA's help in *creating the grandest and most effective campaign ever seen in 1872.* Long-time Republican supporters from the party's anti-slavery inception, the suffragists received no favors for their assistance in getting Grant elected. Instead, a judicial appointee of Grant instructed the jury to find Anthony guilty of voting— for Grant! Gage penned an address to the Republican convention in 1876 asking them to insert a plank in their platform pledging the party *to secure the exercise of this right to all citizens, irrespective of sex.* It was ignored. When Gage presented her suffrage resolution to the party in 1880, the one ally on the Republican platform committee, an African American delegate from Michigan, moved its adoption without success. Four years later (in 1884) the resolutions committee again refused to adopt a plank in their platform giving any recognition to women.

Stanton and Anthony came out with a circular entitled "Stand By the Republican Party" before the election of 1884, and it seemed slightly out of tune with reality. Gage joined the women who supported the idea of forming a woman's party, the Equal Rights Party, advocating equal rights for women, African Americans, Native Americans and immigrants. Belva Lockwood, the first woman to practice law before the Supreme Court and an NWSA member, was their presidential candidate. Although Anthony opposed the party and Stanton would have nothing to do with it, Gage ran as one of the two Electors-at-Large.[37]

It was the second time that Anthony had actively opposed a woman running for president. When broker/editor Victoria Woodhull joined the woman suffrage platform in 1872, she entranced everyone, including Anthony. Woodhull then exposed the fact that the most famous minister in the U.S. was a notorious womanizer. A free love advocate, Woodhull was not put out by Henry Ward Beecher's sexual behavior (he may have been a lover of hers at one time) but, rather, his hypocrisy. As president of the conservative American Woman Suffrage Association, Beecher was heading an organization that publicly denounced the free love beliefs (a woman's right to control her body) of the rival National Woman Suffrage Association, while he privately was having an affair with an officer in the NWSA! Elizabeth Cady Stanton and Matilda Joslyn Gage stood by Woodhull when she was jailed for "obscenity" under the Comstock Act after publishing her revelation about Beecher. Anthony turned her back, and literally turned the lights out on her, shutting down the meeting at which Woodhull announced her candidacy for president right before her arrest.

The protests continued into the 1880s. "The Statue of Liberty is a gigantic lie, a travesty, and a mockery," charged the suffragists when it was unveiled in 1886. "It is the greatest sarcasm of the nineteenth century" to represent liberty as a woman, "while not one single woman throughout the length and breadth of the Land is as yet in possession of political Liberty." The Statue was the ultimate metaphor of the pedestal of powerlessness on which women were placed. The New York Woman Suffrage Association rented a steamer and, protest banners flying, joined the water parade that circled Bedloe (later Ellis) Island during the dedication ceremonies. Neither Stanton nor Anthony was on board. *Ah, women,* Gage dramatically called out in her speech, *I wish I could fill your hearts with a desire for liberty like that which boils in my heart.* [38]

A protest, signed by Anthony, Gage and three other women on behalf of the National Woman Suffrage Association, reminded government officials celebrating the centennial of the Constitution the following year that: "In the midst of the pomps and glories of this celebration women are only onlookers, voiceless and unrepresented, a denial in defiance of the provisions of the Constitution you profess to honor." [39]

In 1888, Stanton finally announced that she'd had it with trying to get support from the political parties, Gage wrote a friend: *She says she has written appeals and protests, declarations, constitutions, speeches, memorials, petitions for half a century and is in the sack-cloth of disfranchisement yet and has no faith left that either party will do anything and cannot trouble herself before these Presidential conventions.* Although Stanton had previously agreed to write the Memorials that year, Gage understood. *Poor dear Mrs. Stanton has been mortified beyond endurance by the rebuffs she has received scarcely enduring the indignity of pleading for rights before men much younger than herself and too, she has met with ingratitude from our own people. I sympathize with her feelings.* [40] Responsibility for the NWSA's documents, previously shared with Stanton, now would fall entirely on Gage, it appeared.

While remaining active politically, Gage also blossomed as a writer during this time. As a correspondent for papers in New York, San Francisco and Syracuse (as well as her local Fayetteville paper), Gage reported the historic events in which she participated: the formation of the NWSA and the Virginia Suffrage Association, Anthony's trial and the presentation of the 1876 *Declaration of Rights of Women* among them. Her publications ranged from an *Appleton's Journal* article about ancient Egyptian female leaders to an encyclopedia entry on the woman's movement.

WOMAN SUFFRAGE TRACTS—NO. 1.

WOMAN AS INVENTOR,

BY

MRS. M. E. JOSLYN GAGE.

ISSUED UNDER THE AUSPICES

OF THE

NEW YORK STATE

WOMAN SUFFRAGE ASSOCIATION.

F. A. DARLING, STEAM BOOK AND JOB PRINTER, FAYETTEVILLE, N. Y.

1870.

Cover, Woman as Inventor *(1870)*

Gage uncovered some remarkable achievements of women that had been ignored or denied by historians. In *Woman as Inventor,* Gage credited Catherine Littlefield Greene, and not Eli Whitney, with the invention of the cotton gin. Greene had the idea but not the mechanical skill to construct it; for that she called on Whitney. When the wooden teeth he used in the original model didn't work, Whitney was ready to abandon the project. Greene convinced him to continue substituting wire teeth and the finished product revolutionized the Southern economy. Greene didn't patent the machine, Gage explained, because *to have done so would have exposed her to the ridicule and contumely of her friends and a loss of position in society, which frowned upon any attempt at outside industry for women.*[41]

In "Who Planned the Tennessee Campaign of 1862?" Gage revealed evidence that Anna Ella Carroll planned the brilliant military strategy that changed the course of the Civil War. The Military Committee of the United States Senate established that Carroll presented an elaborate plan for the campaign to the War Department in late 1861. The Assistant Secretary of War, Thomas A. Scott, and Senator Benjamin F. Wade, Chairman of the Committee on the Conduct of the War, unequivocally stated that Carroll had planned the Tennessee Campaign. That fact was not made public, Senator Wade explained, because, "Mr. Lincoln and Mr. Stanton (the Secretary of War) were opposed to its being known that the armies were moving under the plan of a civilian." *A civilian, and that civilian a woman,* Gage added.[42]

The National Citizen and Ballot Box

IN ADDITION TO her other activities, Gage edited and published the official paper of the NWSA, the *National Citizen and Ballot Box,* from 1878-1881. Each month, chapters of the *History,* movement news and a wide range of topics greeted subscribers to "the cheapest paper in the country" at $1.00 a year. While the "especial object" of the paper was the vote, *advocating the principle that suffrage is the citizen's right and should be protected by national law, it will also touch upon the woman question in all its various aspects,* Gage promised in the Prospectus. The goal of the paper was to *revolutionize the country, striving to make it live up to its fundamental principles.* She delivered on the promises made to her readers, including this one:

> *As the first process toward becoming well is to know you are ill, one of the principle aims of the* **National Citizen** *will be to make those women discontented who are now content, to waken them to self-respect and a desire to use the talents they possess, to educate their consciences aright, to quicken their sense of duty, to destroy morbid beliefs and make them worthy of the life with which their Creator has endowed them.*

Certainly that discontent was fostered by Gage's analysis of the practice of *giving the bride away as a relic of the old barbarism which held daughters as the father's slaves, whom he could sell to any suitor he pleased.* Gage expressed certainty that, with this new understanding, *no self-respecting woman will submit to be given away.*

Building the outrage at injustice of her readers, Gage informed them that rapists seldom went to prison, using the example of Iowa, where, out of fifty-seven rape trials that year, there were only four convictions. One reader offered a major reason why "these crimes go unpunished and are therefore multiplied fearfully." Victims were afraid to bring charges because of knowledge they would, "day after day in the face of a low lived, staring crowd, be compelled to live over again mentally all the horrors of the first outrage. Compelling them to come into open court is but a second outrage inflicted by the State; especially as the law provides that the punishment of the criminal shall depend, not so much upon the proof of his guilt, as upon his inability to hire others to swear that her previous character had been hurt." The standard defense in a rape case rested on establishing, by any means necessary, that the victim had "asked for it."

Several papers, including Brigham Young's *Deseret Evening News* from Salt Lake City objected to Gage's goal of making women discontent. Nonsense, she retorted, *the deepest depth of degradation is reached, when a person who is wronged is insensible of the wrong done him. The most degraded slave of olden time was the one content in his slavery. Whoever would be free, himself must strike the blow,* she concluded. *No blow is ever struck until discontent is felt.*[43]

The paper would befriend *women of every class, condition, rank and name...it matters not how wretched, degraded, fallen they may be,* Gage guaranteed. In reporting the suicide of a well-known prostitute, she blamed the death on *that social system which creates two codes of morals, grading penalties according to the political status of the offender and which, for the same infraction of moral law, allows a man to escape unscathed, while holding a woman to the strictest accountability.*

Gage was outraged that a mother of ten children had been jailed for sixty days for the crime of stealing something for her children to eat, *in food-laden America.* E. H. (Big Bill) Haywood, the union organizer, *rejoiced* at the deep *interest* the paper showed in the labor question. The *hope of the future seems to be largely in cooperation,* Gage felt, sharing success stories of women living collectively and starting cooperative businesses.

Her editorial series on the danger of centralizing the power to control voting in the states attracted *marked attention from the press throughout the Union.*

The paper pledged "a general criticism of men and things" and delivered much of that criticism tongue-in-cheek. When a new Russian sect, the "purifiers," required a husband to confess his sins to his wife once a week, Gage deadpanned, *would not that require a whole week?* A New York boarding house for women required residents to produce endorsements from two "respectable" gentlemen, leading Gage to remind her readers that respectable men *see prostitutes and molest young girls.* These jibes at men gained Gage the reputation of being a "man-hater." When the *Vineland Times* criticized her paper as "too aggressive and too bitter against men," Gage responded good-naturedly:

> *But as to "aggressiveness," bless your soul, that is the way to carry on a warfare. The party only on the defensive is always liable to leave some open point for the enemy's attack. In order*

to accomplish any reform or work in life the way is to be "up and at 'em," and that is what we intend to do and still to preserve love and respect for our father, our husband, our son and all good men. [44]

While Stanton and Parker Pillsbury's the *Revolution* (published by Anthony) lasted only two years, their paper generally appears in suffrage history books, while Gage's newspaper, of twice the duration, is as often ignored. The oversight is significant.

She Who Holds The Sky

I RECEIVED THE NAME of *Ka-ron-ien-ha-wi, or 'Sky Carrier,' or as Mrs. Converse said the Senecas would express it, 'She who holds the sky.'* This is the way Matilda Joslyn Gage described her adoption into the wolf clan of the Mohawk nation in 1893. Her Mohawk sister said *this name would admit me to the Council of Matrons, where a vote would be taken, as to my having a voice in the Chieftainship,* Gage wrote. How amazing this must have been to a woman who went to trial the same year for voting in a school board election. Considered for full voting rights in her adopted nation, she was arrested in her own nation for voting.

While serving as president of the National Woman Suffrage Association eighteen years earlier, Gage wrote a series of articles on the Iroquois for the *New York Evening Post.* "Mrs. Gage, with an exhibition of ardent devotion to the cause of woman's rights...gives prominence to the fact that...the power and importance of women were recognized by the allied tribes," the newspaper commented.

The division of power between the sexes in this Indian republic was nearly equal, Gage wrote. In matters of government...*its women exercised controlling power in peace and war...no sale of lands was valid without consent of the women, while the family relation among the Iroquois demonstrated woman's superiority in power...in the home, the wife was absolute...if the Iroquois husband and wife separated, the wife took with her all the property she had* brought...the children also accompanied the mother, whose right to them was recognized as supreme...never was justice more perfect, never civilization higher.

In the *National Citizen and Ballot Box*, Gage spoke out against the *oppression of Indians* and the government's history of breaking treaties. She exposed the hypocrisy of the white nation denying the right of suffrage to African American and white women, while trying to force citizenship (and suffrage) on Native American men, thereby opening *wide the door to the grasping avarice of the white man*. While supporting the struggle of American Indians to maintain their independent nation status, she compared the social position of white women to that of Indians at the hands of the federal government.

Believing *that the form of government of the United States was borrowed from that of the Six Nations*, Gage concluded *that the modern world is indebted to the Iroquois for its first conception of inherent rights, natural equality of condition, and the establishment of a civilized government upon this basis.*[45]

Gage vowed that her paper *would oppose class legislation of whatever form* and speak out against injustice to any group. She did. Perhaps the most remarkable case is her support of native issues. In the following editorial (May 1878), she demonstrates an understanding of sovereignty and a surprising ability to see beyond the "Christianization and Civilization" policy of church and state toward American Indians (generally supported by progressive non-Indians at the time) to the need to respect treaties.

INDIAN CITIZENSHIP

While the United States is trying to force citizenship upon the Indians, the latter are everywhere protesting against it. The famous Iroquois, or Six Nations, held a council at Onondaga the last of March, upon the old, original council grounds where, before the advent of Columbus, they were wont to meet in settlement of grave questions.

No such important questions ever came up during their old

barbaric life as were discussed at the council in March. First among them was the bill recently introduced in the United States Senate by Mr. Kernan of N.Y., to give those tribes the rights of citizenship and allow them to sell their lands in this State.

The Indians decline the gift of citizenship and although Judge Wallace of the Northern District of New York recently decided in favor of the right of an Oneida Indian who voted at the presidential election of 1876, Chief Skenandoah of the Oneidas was one of the principal speakers against this innovation.

The Mohammeds [Muslims] have a saying that one hour of justice is worth seventy years of prayer; the Indians seem to think one hour of justice worth a thousand years of citizenship, as the drift of their talk was against any law that should either allow or compel them to become citizens, as such a course would open wide the door to the grasping avarice of the white man. They discussed plans to compel the payment due them for lands once deeded them by the United States in treaty but which were afterwards seized and sold for the benefit of our government.

Over one hundred chiefs and warriors of the different nations took part in this discussion. This council of Indians at Onondaga Castle, in the center of the great Empire State, and the convention of the women of the country at Washington in January, the one protesting against citizenship about to be forced upon them, because with it would come further deprivation of their rights,—the other demanding citizenship denied them, in order to protect their rights, are two forcible commentaries upon our so-called republican form of government.

...That the Indians have been oppressed—are now—is true, but the United States has treaties with them, recognizing them as distinct political communities, and duty towards them demands not an enforced citizenship but a faithful living up to its obligations on the part of the Government.

Our Indians are in reality foreign powers, though living among us. With them our country not only has treaty obligations, but pays them, or professes to, annual sums in consideration of such treaties; the U.S. Government paying the Iroquois their annuities in June, the

State of New York in September. One great aversion the Iroquois have
to citizenship is that they would then be compelled to pay taxes,
which they look upon as a species of tribute. From an early day they
were accustomed to receiving tribute, sending among the conquered
tribes of Long Island for their annual dues of wampum. As poor, as
oppressed as they are, surrounded as they now are by the conquering
white man, they still preserve their olden spirit of independence, still
look upon themselves as distinct nations and in the payment of their
annuities, fancy they are receiving, as of old, tribute from their
enemies. Compelling them to become citizens would be like the
forcible annexation of Cuba, Mexico, or Canada to our government,
and as unjust.

A delegation of Indians called at the White House on New Year's
day. As a sarcasm of justice, on their "Happy New Year" cards
were inscribed extracts from various treaties made with them, and
disregarded rights guaranteed them in treaty by the Government.

The women of the nation might take hint from the Indians and
on July 4th, send to the legislative, judicial and executive bodies,
cards inscribed with such sentiments as "Governments derive their
just powers from the consent of the governed." "Taxation without
representation is tyranny," and others of like character.

The black man had the right of suffrage conferred upon him
without his asking for it, and now an attempt is made to force it upon
the red man in direct opposition to his wishes, while women citizens,
already members of the nation, to whom it rightfully belongs, are
denied its exercise. Truly, consistency is a jewel so rare its only abode
is the toad's head.

While her analysis of racial oppression was astute, her writing
still reflects the popular image of the "savage Indian," as this passage
demonstrates:

Can woman's political degradation reach much lower depth?
She, educated, enlightened, Christian, in vain begs for the
crumbs cast contemptuously aside by savages. While some of
these red men are educated Christians, others still cling to their

pagan rites, yearly celebrating the Green Corn Dance, yearly burning the White Dog.

After close of the council its younger members indulged in a war dance, and, scalping knife in hand, with painted faces, whirling tomahawk and shrieking war-whoop, recounted their old time prowess. [46]

Gage saw a long way. Her vision, however, wasn't perfect.

Religion

I WANT YOU to bring my revolver and cartridges; have them serviced, Gage instructed her son from Philadelphia in 1876. Her friends, Judge and Mrs. Westbrook, were armed. Mob violence from the religious conservatives was predicted because the Philadelphia Exhibition was opening on a Sunday, the day they believed should be a legislated day of rest.[47] While the gun proved unnecessary, for the rest of her life Gage would battle the religious right over their attempt to merge church and state. Among their seemingly innocuous proposals was enforced Sunday rest.

Stanton consistently argued that public buildings should remain open on Sunday to allow working people, who worked seven days a week, to visit. Gage agreed and clarified the political agenda they both knew hid behind the issue. If the "political religion," as Gage described Christianity, forced the entire nation to practice their religious observance of Sunday rest, freedom of religion would be destroyed. During the centennial year, Gage attended the founding meeting of the free-thought Liberal League, choosing the side of religious freedom in this fight and committing to the most important work of her life.

"She looks anything but a reformer," the *New York Herald* said about Gage two years later when she spoke at her first freethinker convention. She "is more like a loving grandmother with a room full of grandchildren. She was dressed in black velvet, with passamenterie lace and silk trimming. Her plentiful white hair was combed into a

Matilda Joslyn Gage at age 54 (1880)

great bunch at the back of her head. She constantly played with a fan during her speech," the paper described. The contrast between her demeanor and words must have been startling. This elegantly dressed, white-haired woman charged that hatred of women was the centerpiece of Christianity:

> The Christian Church is based upon...the theory that woman brought sin and death into the world, and that therefore she was punished by being placed in a condition of inferiority to man—a condition of subjection, of subordination. This is the foundation today of the Christian Church.

When the police arrested a woman—under the Comstock laws—for selling a birth control manual at this convention, Gage placed the arrest in a larger context, as she was so good at doing. Underlying the opposition to giving women information on the prevention of pregnancy was the deeper fear of giving women the tools for autonomy. The Church was determined that woman should not have control of her body, or the fruits thereof, in any manner. *Do you know that every woman here who chances to be a married woman has the same danger of arrest if she dare to claim her child for her own?* Gage asked the audience. In preventing or creating children, it made no difference. Woman was to be subordinate in either case.[48]

While still a leader in suffrage work, Gage began to believe that no single concern was as important to women as religion. From the beginning of the movement, the church had been the major opponent of the suffragist's demand for full personhood. The Christian argument against women's rights stayed basically the same through Gage's life. The General Association of Congregational ministers of Massachusetts issued an 1837 Pastoral Letter in response to women's anti-slavery work, which set the model. Warning of "the dangers which at present seem to threaten the female character with widespread and permanent injury," the ministerial association went on to clarify woman's God-ordained role:

> "The appropriate duties and influence of woman are clearly stated in the New Testament...The power of woman is her

dependence, flowing from the consciousness of that weakness which God has given her for her protection…We appreciate the unostentatious prayers and efforts of woman in advancing the cause of religion…But when she assumes the place and tone of man as a public reformer…she yields the power which God has given her for her protection, and her character becomes unnatural."

God created woman, in short, to be a clinging vine.

"If the vine, whose strength and beauty is to lean upon the trellis-work, and half conceal its clusters, thinks to assume the independence and the overshadowing nature of the elm, it will not only cease to bear fruit, but fall in shame and dishonor into the dust."[49]

The church provided the theological justification for woman's inferior state by teaching that woman was made to be subordinate to man. Further, by naming woman as the source of evil, responsible for the downfall of humanity through Eve's original sin, the church set woman up to be the victim of man. The story of Eve was not peripheral to Christianity; it was *its corner stone; for, without the doctrine of the fall, and the consequent need of a Savior, the whole Christian super-structure drops into nothingness,* Gage insisted. It seemed obvious to her that as long as Christian dogma shaped women's lives, they would never be free.

The "political religion" must be fought politically, she decided, and Gage introduced a series of resolutions that were adopted at the 1878 NWSA convention:

RESOLVED: That as the duty of every individual is self-development, the lessons of self-sacrifice and obedience taught women by the Christian church have been fatal not only to her own highest interests, but through her have also dwarfed and degraded the race.

RESOLVED: That the fundamental principle of the Protestant reformation, the right of individual conscience and judgment in the interpretation of Scripture, heretofore conceded to and exercised by men alone, should now be claimed by woman and that in her most vital interests she should no longer trust authority, but be guided by her own reason.

RESOLVED: That it is through the perversion of the religious element in woman, cultivating the emotions at the expense of her reason, playing upon her hopes and fears of the future, holding this life with all its high duties forever in abeyance to that which is to come, that she and the children she has trained, have been so completely subjugated by priest-craft and superstition.

Clergymen and press denounced the resolutions, the *New York World* declaring, "Never was there a clearer illustration of the evil tendencies of the Woman's Rights movement." Lucy Stone's husband, Henry Blackwell, was highly critical of the resolutions in the AWSA paper, the *Woman's Journal.* Gage responded to this entire outcry:

Every woman suffragist from the commencement has been bombarded with Paul, knocked on the head by somebody else's interpretation of the Scriptures, and branded as heretical. We are tired of this. We know our rights, and knowing them, we shall dare maintain them. What is still more, we know the facts of history, and we know the present degraded condition of woman today is due to that interpretation of Scripture, which holds— always has held—that she had no right to live for herself, and to think for herself. [50]

When four women were expelled from the Congregational Church for their women's rights activities the next year (1879), Gage insisted that the NWSA advance and not retreat in the face of the enemy. When some women expressed fear that the organization would be further denounced from the pulpit as anti-Christian, Gage asked, *if things had come to the pass that a threat of the attacks of the clergy was to be held over the convention to deter it from doing its duty?* Rising to the challenge, the NWSA passed her next set of resolutions by a very large vote:

WHEREAS, By false interpretation of Scripture, woman is held to duties, not rights; responsibilities, not power; and is deemed to be an appendage to man, created for his benefit and happiness.

WHEREAS, This interpretation has nourished in man, love of dominion, selfishness and sensuality, and has humiliated and degraded woman and humanity; therefore,

RESOLVED: That woman was created a free, responsible human being, equal to man in rights, powers, duties and obligations; that among her rights is an equal right with man to a private interpretation of Scripture, to self-development and self-government in home, church and state.[51]

Gage was formulating a two-fold analysis:

First, the foundation of woman's oppression is the church.

Second (and most startling), the foundation upon which the church rests is the oppression of women. Paul—*who engrafted his belief and polity upon the nascent Church,* and whose *doctrines have corrupted the truths of nature, crushed the efforts of science, and made of the Church a male theocracy*—was the chief villain, she maintained.

International Council of Women

T HE NWSA SENT 10,000 invitations to women's rights workers from around the world to come to Washington for a discussion of their common concerns in the spring of 1888. Gage, Stanton and Anthony were among the seven planners, although Stanton was in Europe until the last minute, and did very little work to organize it. Gage spoke three times, and chaired one session.

The Lord's Prayer opened the Sunday afternoon Religious Symposium and Anthony introduced Gage, her longtime friend and coworker, to speak on *Woman in the Early Christian Church.* A murmur went up from the crowd of women. "There is not in all the body of women gathered on the platform of the International Council one whose life and acts are more bound up in its progress and influence than Matilda Joslyn Gage," one newspaper had proclaimed.

Gage had gained a reputation for four qualities. She was principled to a fault. She was brilliant. She was fearless in stating her beliefs. And she did not suffer fools gladly. Gage proceeded to live up to her reputation by introducing *a subject of profound surprise and astonishment* to her during the Council: *the almost total ignoring of the Divine Motherhood of God by those who have in any way referred to the Supreme Power.* Being required to open an earlier session over which she had presided with a prayer, *I was in some little trouble to find the woman far enough advanced in theology to recognize the divine motherhood,* Gage continued.

*All thoughtful persons, **and foremost among them should be the women here represented,*** she chastised the Council delegates, *must be aware of the historical fact that the prevailing religious idea in regard to woman has been the base of all their restrictions and degradation. It underlies political, legal, educational, industrial, and social disabilities of whatever character and nature.* Gage made no attempt to mask her disgust at women who would gather to discuss their oppression, and then honor the very religious beliefs that were the cause of that oppression. *Inasmuch as history teaches us that the rack, the torture, the destruction of human will, the degradation of woman for the past eighteen hundred years, have been dependent upon masculine interpretation of the Bible, based upon belief in a purely masculine divinity,* she reproached the audience, *this Council has been to me a dangerous evidence of woman's ignorance upon this most important of questions.*

Not a new notion, the idea of a female god was, in fact, the world's oldest, she reminded her audiences: *In all ancient nations we find goddesses seated everywhere with gods, in many instances regarded as superior to them, and of greater influence in the affairs of the universe.* Even in the early Christian church, *the equal feminine nature of the divine was accepted.*

The Bible creation story, Gage said, should read: *So God, Father-Mother, created man, male and female created He-She. Eve,* she went on, *means the one who holds or gives life, the life-giver, the creative principle, in which respect the woman possesses superi-ority over the man.*

The early church, however, proceeded to totally remove woman from this position of spiritual authority, and *while in word proclaiming the unity of God, had in reality passed over to idolatry in a worship of the masculine.*

Gage concluded on a hopeful note, proclaiming that, *the world is in the midst of a tremendous religious revolution* and heralding the dawn of a new age in which *Man has lost his power over woman, against whose moral and material rights the interpretations of the Bible and the whole force of the church have been directed for nearly 2,000 years.* [52]

Her words electrified the audience, and galvanized the like-minded. Women swarmed the platform, declaring the speech "magnificent." Clara Colby, editor of the *Woman's Tribune,* promised, "I will print it entire and give you immortality." Virginia Minor teased that she would oppose Gage's election as chair of the NWSA's executive committee since the speech would "render her immortal" and that was enough. Women kissed their hands to her from other tables and clasped her about the waist in thanks since "that was what they had hungered for," and they feared that no one would have the courage to say it at the Council.

Gage privately explained to her children that she had rewritten the speech *after I saw the pious way of the council — the ignorant nonsense of some of these women.* She was referring, no doubt, to Frances Willard, the President of the Women's Christian Temperance Union (WCTU), who she had directly targeted in her speech, charging:

> *It is especially surprising that the advocates of social purity fail to recognize the femininity of the divine…Had it not been for this theory which has grown out of the doctrines of the church in regard to the masculinity of God and the supreme wickedness of woman, the world would not now be filled with the grossness and moral wrongs which, because of her higher nature, are every-where made to fall with supreme force upon woman.*

"To speak of atrocious crimes in mild language is treason to virtue," Burke said. The cost of this unswerving truth telling, of course, is generally the sort of isolation and neutralizing that Gage ultimately experienced. Not in this moment, however; but the seeds were sown.

Of course, but a small part of my radicalism appeared in that speech, Gage explained to her family, *only enough to rouse enquiry in those groveling material minds.* The Council showed her the importance of writing the full extent of her radicalism. *I want to be alone & have rest, & write,* she resolved, *to finish my book which is my first important work.* Gage held no illusions about the reception that she would receive. *I expect it will bring a storm of indignation & vituperation onto me,* she acknowledged to her children, *but I deem its completion a duty I owe the world.* Five years later, *Woman, Church and State* would be in print.[53]

During those long, painful years, Gage would wage an unsuccessful battle to keep the conservatives from taking control of the movement. Failing this, she would form an anti-church organization—her mail intercepted by the government—and lose her position and most of her friends of forty years in the movement. The seeds of all this were sown at the International Council of Women.

Throughout the Council sessions, Gage watched the WCTU President, Frances Willard, dazzle audiences with her charisma. Behind the scenes, she saw Willard's powerful ability to sway decisions. When Willard was elected President of the National Council of Women, an organization that grew out of the Council, Gage's concern turned to alarm. The Council *opened my eyes as never before,* Gage wrote to Stanton, explaining:

> *The great dangerous organization of the movement is the WCTU; and Frances Willard, with her magnetic force, her power of leadership, her desire to introduce religious tests into the government, is the most dangerous person upon the American continent today. You and I must stand firm; we have a great tide to stem, a great battle yet before us...Get ready for a strong fight.*[54]

The Women's Christian Temperance Union was an army of "organized mother-love" under the banner, "For God and Home and Native Land" going into battle, initially, against the liquor traffic. They tried praying and singing, but these tactics proved rather unsuccessful. Frances Willard then received divine inspiration (she said) to work for suffrage so women could vote liquor out of existence. She joined the American Woman Suffrage Association, as did many WCTU members.

Why suffrage? Temperance simply opened the door. Her agenda went far beyond, as Willard admitted in 1888:

"The Woman's Christian Temperance Union, local, state, national, world-wide, has one vital, organic thought, one absorbing purpose, one underlying enthusiasm. It is that Christ shall be this world's King. King of its courts, its camps, and its commerce; King of its colleges and its cloisters; King of its customs and its constitutions."[55]

The WCTU plan was to make prayers mandatory in the public schools, to force the closure of all public activities on the Sabbath, and, most importantly, to change the Constitution to have Christ recognized *as the author and head of government.* The last goal was the most frightening of all to Gage, who was concerned that it would create a political test under which public office could only be held *by such as fear God.* She warned, *This looks like a return to the Middle Ages and proscription for religious opinions, and is the great danger of the hour.* Stanton, who was also alarmed, worried that: "These women do not seem to see that all this special legislation about faith, Sabbaths, drinking, etc., etc., is the entering wedge to general governmental interference which would eventually subject us to an espionage that would soon become tyrannical in the extreme."[56]

The WCTU's threat to merge church and state was not an idle one. It was part of a right-wing movement that was sweeping the country. Bills were introduced in Congress requiring school prayers and a closure of all public facilities on Sunday. Supported by the WCTU, a Prohibition Party sprang up with a Preamble proclaiming "Almighty God as the source of all power in government." One of their platforms called for the establishment of uniform national laws governing marriage and divorce. The struggle to gain the right to divorce was in full swing, some state victories having been won against the Christian dogma that marriage was a divine union which could not be broken. A uniform national law established by Christian conservatives would undoubtedly be based upon their religious beliefs: the word "obey" would be mandatory in the marriage ceremony for women, and divorce, even if a woman's life was in danger from a battering husband, would be prohibited. The Prohibition party also included a suffrage plank, calling for the states (not the federal government) to restore the right of suffrage to all who would meet *moral and educational qualifications,* the *moral evidently to be twisted church-wise,* Gage warned.

Willard stepped into the political arena, saying: "Concerning the platform of our next national Prohibition Convention, I am content to leave it substantially as it is, save that it should declare Christ and his law to be the true basis of government, and the supreme authority, in national as in individual life."

The WCTU wanted the vote for reasons opposite those of the NWSA, as one woman explained: "I am a woman suffragist through and through, because I believe in human rights, in human liberty. The orthodox party are woman suffragists because they want to get the power to suppress both."[57]

Anthony liked Willard. Not only that, Anthony was coming to believe more and more that the only important issue was the vote, and that any woman who supported suffrage—for whatever reason—was an ally. Stanton and Gage were rapidly moving in a different political direction from their old ally. As the political distance between them grew, the gap between Anthony and the AWSA closed.

Gage took action, moving back into a leadership position in the NWSA to try to stem the tide of religious conservatism that she saw sweeping the movement. She explained her course of action to her confidante, her son: *When I refused the nomination of Chairman of the Executive Committee again in 1881, at Boston, it was because I felt that younger persons ought to do the hard work that had been mine for years, & so I nominated my own successor. But this spring the pressure upon me to take it again was very strong, and as I recognized the crucial position of the Association, I allowed my name to stand. After the first meeting of Apr. 5th of five hours, I tried to resign, as I felt the hard work it would be—but was overwhelmingly voted down—& so I am in the place which requires a strong, steady hand, with money at command.*

Gage went on: *Our Association has been steered into an orthodox pit-hole by Miss. Anthony & her aids—and it needs not only a strong will, but money to put us back. You would scarcely believe that even Mrs. Stanton has been dictated to & outrageously treated by Susan and some of her young aids. She has both **told** me & **voted** me in regard to it. The opposition has money and spends it freely. I have brains, will & the sustaining hand of many.*[58]

To one of those supporters she wrote, *Great watchfulness and great circumspection is needed, as we are [swamped]. Orthodoxy and social recognition are our great enemies. I fear, yet hope. Write me as you see necessary.*[59]

Merger and Betrayal

ANTHONY AND Lucy Stone held a secret meeting to discuss merging their two organizations. When the plan surfaced, Gage found the idea absurd. The two groups were as different as night and day. The issues that Stanton and Gage considered the real ones—woman's oppression by the church, the state, the capitalist and the home, and the need to destroy all four institutions—did not resonate with the AWSA. The vote was an end in itself, as the AWSA saw it, while for Gage, Stanton, and the other radical women of the NWSA, it was simply the tool by which to lift this four-fold oppression women suffered.

When NWSA members committed civil disobedience by voting, the AWSA spoke out against the tactic. They disassociated themselves from the NWSA's presentation of the *Woman's Declaration* in 1876. The two groups had a long history of working at cross-purposes. The NWSA was demanding a constitutional amendment to *protect* women from the states that were illegally denying them suffrage. At the same time, the AWSA was *asking* states to give women the vote, thereby telling these states that they had the right to confer suffrage. The AWSA maintained that only states could determine suffrage. The NWSA believed that this position wasn't only unconstitutional, but it also undermined the national foundation of our government, by taking from the federal government the power to protect the fundamental rights of citizenship.

The final straw was the AWSA alliance with WCTU members including Frances Willard, "the most dangerous person in America." How could the NWSA, which regularly passed resolutions declaring that church teachings were at the basis of woman's oppression, consider uniting with a group which had as members women who were working to make those church teachings the basis of the government?[60]

Gage was chair of the Executive Committee of the NWSA in 1888 when the merger proposal from the AWSA came in. The Conference Committee, which was created by the NWSA to respond to the union plan, responded with a counter proposal. The NWSA and AWSA would meet in joint convention to work out the details of union with one vote for every twenty-five members of each Association. The actions of this convention would be binding on both groups. The results of this plan were obvious, since the NWSA membership far outnumbered that of the AWSA. Predictably, the AWSA declined the offer, stating that the larger organization "could impose whatever terms it chose, thus simply obliterating the other society."[61]

There matters stood going into the 1889 NWSA annual Washington convention, as far as Gage knew. She hadn't counted on two things. Stanton's indifference and Anthony's duplicity. Those two things would change the course of the history of the woman's rights movement.

Anthony had received a new offer from the AWSA, which she was determined to push through the upcoming convention. She did not notify Gage of this offer or of the fact that it would be acted upon at the convention. Gage, as chair of the Executive Committee, should have been informed of any important items that would come before that body, and took it on faith that she would be. Anthony, who unofficially controlled the purse strings of the movement through the many bequests that came to the NWSA in her name, knew that Gage was visiting her children in Dakota and needed travel money to get back to Washington. Travel money was always freely given, to Gage and any other women who needed it, but this year Anthony offered to pay only a part of Gage's expenses. Unable to afford the trip, Gage did not come to the 1889 convention.

Anthony presided over the Executive Committee meetings in Gage's absence. She announced receipt of the new AWSA union offer and "as she supposed no one would question her right to do so," she appointed the members of a committee to consider the merger proposal. When only one woman questioned her authority[6], Anthony set up her committee, made up primarily of those who openly favored union. Two members who opposed the merger were asked by Anthony and May Wright Sewall to resign on the grounds that a person whose mind was made up against the union was not a proper member of the committee. However, no one who was in favor of union was asked to leave, while two others who declared themselves in favor of union were added to the committee after it convened. One of these women refused to serve on the committee when she found out what was going on.

As the convention drew to a close at eleven o'clock on the night of the final session, Anthony's committee brought a new constitution before the floor of the convention for endorsement. Most of the out-of-town members had already left for home and the remaining group of tired and unsuspecting women approved the new constitution without giving it much thought. The union committee immediately went to the executive committee, which was finishing up its business, and announced that the NWSA convention had just endorsed a new constitution. Since this constitution had previously been approved by the AWSA, they argued, nothing stood in the way of merger now. A motion was introduced that the NWSA unite with the AWSA.

The union advocates were united and tightly organized to push through the merger while those opposed to it were stunned, confused and disbelieving. Clara Colby moved that the question be submitted to a mail vote of all NWSA members. Anthony's union "cabal" strongly opposed this idea, "on the grounds that nobody knew anything about the division, and it would only set them to wondering." The NWSA membership would never submit to such a union, Harriette Shattuck declared, as evidenced by the large number of letters the convention had received opposing any possibility of merger. The only opposition came from the very old workers who carried grudges over old grievances, an advocate of merger retorted. Shattuck replied that she "was a young worker" and the grievances weren't old: it "was not three weeks since National methods had been slandered and opposed" in an article in the AWSA paper entitled, "Congress Has No Jurisdiction."

There may have been only two women who had the personal power and credibility to stand up to the authority of Anthony. Stanton had washed her hands of the fate of the NWSA and Gage sat in South Dakota. Caught off guard, some of the women who opposed union, like Isabella Beecher Hooker, began to capitulate. The merger seemed inevitable. With the constitution changed, the demoralized women realized that the old organization didn't even exist anymore. Colby's motion to turn the decision over to the NWSA membership was defeated. The question of union was placed before this midnight session of the Executive Committee. It passed by a vote of 30 to 11.

In the months that followed, many members of the NWSA wrote to Gage, shocked and angry. They had not given their consent to this union; it had taken place with no prior warning. At their request, Gage wrote a formal protest to the merger.

A union in name is valueless without a union in spirit, she wrote, *and there is less real union now than there was before the formal union took place.* She exposed the *unjustifiable methods* used to effect the union, including the fact that the AWSA had put the decision to a vote of its full membership, while the NWSA had not. The union cabal had violated the very principle for which they were all working: the consent of the governed. Gage called for the committee to be held accountable for their actions:

> *Having thus trampled under foot the individual rights of members of the National Woman Suffrage Association, the "thirty," (suggestive number) have forfeited all claim to be considered representative of, or even as belonging to that Association.*[62]

Examining the new constitution, Gage realized that it had insidiously removed the structure that had focused the NWSA on working toward a national suffrage amendment. Where members had previously joined as individuals, they now had to join a state organization, and could only come into the national organization if they were chosen as delegates from their state. The state delegate structure of the AWSA replaced personal representation. This changed the very nature of their work from a national to a state focus, and disfranchised all the NWSA members except those chosen as state delegates. *By adoption of this Constitution and change in method of work, the National Woman Suffrage Association has been virtually destroyed,* Gage wrote. This was no union, bad as that would have been. This was worse. Anthony and her ring had destroyed the NWSA, created a state-focused suffrage organization out of its remains, and turned that organization over to the AWSA.

Five NWSA officers joined Gage in signing the Protest and she mailed it to every NWSA member. If the membership wanted to stop the union, they now had the information on which to act. *The full extent of the treachery by which we were sold has not yet been fathomed and maybe never will, and will not be unless persons cast aside all preferences for, and blind belief in some who were prominent in this "union,"* Gage wrote to a member of the Executive Committee.[63] She was of course referring to Anthony, and the worshipful reverence of the young women who followed her every wish, referring to her as "Saint Susan."

Anger at Anthony was widespread. Many, including Stanton, believed she had sold out the NWSA to the conservative AWSA-WCTU women with the promise that she would be the first President of the united organization. The charges reached Anthony's ears and she responded defensively to Olympia Brown:

> "I suppose your feeling of my change is the same as that of Mrs.
> Gage and Mrs. Stanton—that is because I am not as intolerant of
> the so-called Christian women as they are—that therefore I have
> gone, or am about to go over to the popular church. I do not
> approve of their system of fighting the religious dogmas of the
> people I am trying to convert to my doctrine of equal rights to
> women. But if they can afford to distrust my religious integrity,
> I can afford to let them."[64]

Woman's National Liberal Union

GAGE HAD DONE what she could to stop the merger.
The membership knew the way in which it had been
accomplished, and its consequences. It was now up to
them to act. Realistically, the amount of energy it would require to
undo the damage could probably not be mobilized. Stanton threw up
her hands in disgust, believing the worst had already happened:

> "The National Association has been growing politic and
> conservative for some time. Lucy and Susan alike see suffrage
> only. They do not see woman's religious and social bondage.
> Neither do the young women in either association, hence they
> may as well combine for they have one mind and one purpose."[65]

Anthony was worried that the NWSA women who opposed the
merger would organize and try to stop it at the union convention. In
anticipation, she organized her troops, writing to old friends and
acquaintances all over the country asking them to "Come and stand
by Susan once more." [66] She needn't have bothered, for most of the
women were afraid to confront her and many simply dropped out of
the movement, disillusioned.

With Stanton turning her back on the situation, and Anthony's
dogged single-minded determination, it must have seemed hopeless
to Gage to try to undo the merger. Corresponding with women

around the country about the combined dangers of the WCTU and the merger, Gage became convinced that the time had come to provide leadership in another direction.

"I'm sick of the song of suffrage," Stanton had repeatedly told Gage. Her focus was changing, she explained, "as I have passed from the political to the religious phrase of this question, I now see more clearly than ever, that the arch enemy to woman's freedom skulks behind the altar." They agreed that the most important work at hand was to oppose the anti-woman dogma of the church. As Stanton put it: "to rouse woman to a sense of her degradation under the canon law and church discipline, is the work that interests me most, and to which I prepare to devote the sunset of my life."

The work was especially critical now, with the increasing threat to freedom posed by the WCTU, and that organization's ties to the AWSA. A dramatic change in Stanton's thinking occurred. This woman who had stood tight in the face of terrible opposition since she introduced the original woman suffrage resolution at the first woman's rights convention over forty years before now saw a more important issue. "I would rather live under a government of men alone with religious liberty than under a mixed government without it," Stanton was saying.

For several years the two women had been talking about forming an anti-church organization. Gage believed it was time and Stanton agreed, but she would not make any commitment to get involved in a leadership role. "I will join and speak when you say I must," she told Gage, but she was tired of political work, and "would not take any office in any organization" ever again.[67] She lied.

When the National-American Woman Suffrage Association (NAWSA), the merged organization, held their founding convention four months later, in February 1890, Stanton gratefully accepted the office of president. Anthony engineered her election. We may never know what transpired behind the scenes, but we can speculate. As Anthony faced charges that she had brought about the merger so that she could lead the combined forces, it may have seemed in her interest to support Stanton for president. Over the past years, Stanton had spent increasingly more time in England and had less concern with the organizational work, becoming a figurehead president of the NWSA. Anthony had run the organization behind the scenes. They could simply continue that arrangement. After years of conflict with Lucy Stone and Henry Blackwell, assuming the presidency of an organization merging their two groups must have been a sweet victory for Stanton.

Stanton often acted impulsively, and perhaps she didn't think through the compromise with her principles she'd have to make in assuming the presidency of the NAWSA. She quickly learned. When asked about her connection with Gage's new organization which met in convention the following week, Stanton replied that, as the NAWSA President, she "could not honorably lend my name or influence to what is in the nature of a secession from the suffrage ranks."[68]

Gage was devastated. This casual betrayal of the political vision she and Stanton had shared, and for which they had worked for over twenty years, was beyond her comprehension. While she might be outspoken and tactless, Gage was as good as her word. "She was absolutely honest in all her dealings, and I would take her word at any time as against anybody else's," one co-worker said.[69] Not being capable of such an act, Gage could not understand how someone could turn away from a commitment they had made or abandon their beliefs in this way. Deeply injured, Gage nevertheless turned to the work at hand.

Anthony was fearful that Gage's new organization would draw women from her suffrage cause, and she denounced the Woman's National Liberal Union as "ridiculous, absurd, sectarian, bigoted and too horrible for anything," in letters to women across the country. She forbade her followers to attend Gage's convention.[70] So did Henry Blackwell, as Gage wrote her son: *Susan & Blackwell counsel or **forbid** attendance upon my convention. Mrs. Stanton has behaved the worst of them all as I will write when I have time. We shall succeed.*[71]

Succeed she did. Despite Anthony's best attempt to stop Gage's organization, the women came from all over the country to attend the founding convention of the Woman's National Liberal Union.

With only four months planning, there were thirty-three states represented. Especially mortifying to Anthony must have been the fact that the WNLU's convention received more news coverage than did the founding convention of the NAWSA the week before. *I have some of the best Washn. reportorial staff on this side,* Gage informed her son, *and have been interviewed & interviewed.*

The WNLU brought together a range of radical reformers. Suffragists, labor organizers, anarchists, freethinkers and prison reformers all found common cause in an absolute separation of church and state. The organization opposed prayer or religious instruction in the public schools. The church held full responsibility for woman's oppression, the group agreed. Gage pronounced their resolutions *the broadest & most defiant (& "grandest" the friends say) of any that were ever put forth.* Never expecting anyone to accept anything on faith, she told her son, *You will judge for yourself:*

That the Christian Church, of whatever name, is based on the theory that woman was created secondary and inferior to man, and brought sin into the world and necessitated the sacrifice of a Savior.

That Christianity is false and its foundation a myth, which every discovery of science shows to be as baseless as its former belief that the earth is flat.

That every Church is the enemy of liberty and progress and the chief means of enslaving woman' s conscience and reason, and, therefore, as the first and most necessary step toward her emancipation, we should free her from the bondage of the Church.

Gage described the process by which she decided to go directly after the church:

*I did not at first think of attacking the **foundations** of the church itself—but was thinking one day, when a sudden light came into my mind—an illumination—which said '**the church**'—and then I knew it was right. People wrote me…to say ecclesiasticism,* *sacerdotalism etc. etc. I thought it all carefully over, & knew I meant **the church** itself & I said so. I think there was never in the world such a step taken before. I am as much as ever, a believer in the **invisible** church—but **not** in this rotten thing known to the world as "the Christian Church."* [72]

At a time when the country had entered a period of great conservatism, the Woman's National Liberal Union provided a base for progressive activists. The convention spoke with many voices. The president of the Woman's Industrial League talked about the problems of working women. Voltairine de Cleyre, one of the best-known anarchists in America, proclaimed:

> "For myself, I shall oppose not only the union of church and state, but the actuating authority that lies back of both of them. Economic independence (the right of every human being to his share of the world's inheritance)…gained, the politician will be out of work."

There was a good deal of talk about the economic injustice of the legal system, under which only the rich could receive a fair hearing. William Aldrich, who supported the development of a system of public defenders, declared:

> "This government of the people, by the people, and for the people, seems to be very much limited in the interpretation of the word people; the poor, the women—both married and single—the children, the Indians and other unfortunate inhabitants are not people; the phrase should be changed to read, a government of rich men, by rich men, for rich men." [73]

At a time when the country was moving rapidly toward the right, it was a bold act to bring together representatives of the most radical groups in a frontal assault on Christianity. Not surprisingly, the backlash was swift and widespread. Almost immediately, a sermon was preached against Gage and the WNLU at the Sixth Presbyterian Church in Washington, D.C. Gage was pleased: *I am glad of it. I wish to compel thought and attract attention to the new step.*[74] Clergymen in Iowa and Massachusetts joined in and *hurled their anathemas against this association, as inimical to Bible morality, and especially against the women leading in this step.* A Catholic orphanage required the 700 children in their care to pray against these *demoralizing ideas.* The government intercepted and opened the mail of the women leaders of the WNLU.[75]

The hardest part was the loss of friends. Having challenged Anthony and lost the struggle for the direction of the movement, Gage found old friends falling away. Her earliest and most intimate associates "almost if not quite without exception...abandoned her and cast out even her name as an unclean thing," her old friend Parker Pillsbury accused.[76]

The outpouring of support from allies matched the attack of her enemies, and must have eased the loss of friends and coworkers. Gage wrote when she returned home from the convention:

> *I have letters from all parts of the country rejoicing in my work— one from a fruit-grower of Southern California since I came home, & one from Georgia & to-day one from Missouri & one from Michigan—all asking what they can do to help. A letter from a lady physician of Phila, while I was in Wash. contained $5 & said a society of 138 were with her—one from Maine while in W said 100 persons wished to join.*

Within a few months, the response had spread internationally:

> *I have been asked for my photograph...to go to Sweden with a sketch of my life. An article of mine is about [to appear] in a Swedish paper. I just received an English Freethought paper containing extracts from my speech at the late convention.*[77]

Gage called this convention her *grandest, most courageous work.* The work, however, had only begun and Gage feared that she didn't have the resources to keep it going.

> *I need double the time I have & double the strength to attend to this business. If I could only make fifty of myself, I could perform*

wonders. I am now printing paper & envelopes & 5,000 leaflets. Shall soon publish a full report in pamphlet form, & other things. What I need is abundance of money, to hire a secretary & typewriter—things look so bad for me and I am so hard up most of the time I don't know just what I can or ought to do.[78]

The organization, begun with such promise, died from inadequate resources. Gage published the convention report and brought out one issue of the *Liberal Thinker,* a newspaper for the organization. Nothing more was heard from it. What the church couldn't accomplish, lack of money did.

The voice of Matilda Joslyn Gage, however, wasn't silenced. Three years later it would come forth with even greater strength.

Woman, Church and State

E VEN IF I SHOULD slip out, my chief life work, my **Woman, Church and State** *is done, ready for the printer,* Gage wrote her son in February 1893. The book was on the market by July, published by the Socialist firm of Charles Kerr in Chicago. The cloth edition sold for $2.00 and a half-leather cover cost $3.00. The book caused quite a stir and received surprisingly favorable reviews for a book so far in advance of its time. Freethinkers, of course, loved it. A California professor predicted that it would "rank among the memorable and classic works of all time." Victoria Woodhull (Martin's) English magazine, the *Humanitarian,* applauded the "vigor and directness with which Gage swept away the theological cobwebs which for ages have obscured the light," while a Swedish fan offered to translate it into his native tongue.

"The work cannot fail to command attention among thinkers," predicted the *Chicago Times.* The *Philadelphia Press* called it "an earnest and eloquent book," and the *Boston Transcript* said that it was "perhaps the fullest and strongest presentation of the case from the radical woman's standpoint." Even the *Kansas Farmer* approved, telling its readers, "it is a revelation and ought to be read extensively."[79]

"Mrs. Gage is one of a trio—Elizabeth Cady Stanton and Susan B. Anthony being the others—whose names are household words among the workers for and supporters of woman suffrage,"[80] the *Truth Seeker* reminded its readers when reviewing *Woman, Church and State.* Gage put a quick end to the connection:

> *I hope that no future mention of either **Mrs. Stanton** or **Miss Anthony** will be made. I have suffered **too much** at their hands to wish to advertize them in any way. If W.C.& S. cannot stand on its own merits let it fall. I have forbidden Mr. Kerr to ever mention those women in connection with me—ever again. They have stabbed me in reputation, and Susan, at least, has stolen in money from me. They are traitors, also, to woman's highest needs—and Mrs. Stanton, especially, I look upon in woman's battle for freedom, as I do on Benedict Arnold during the war of the Revolution;—she is a traitor to what she knows is right.*[81]

Gage presented a copy of the book to the school library in her hometown of Fayetteville, New York. Thomas W. Sheedy, who was prominent in the local Roman Catholic Church, sat on the school board. Taking one look at the book, he immediately sent it to Anthony Comstock, chief enforcer of the obscenity laws bearing his name, asking him to render an opinion on the book. Comstock threatened to arrest the school board members if they placed the book in the school library:

> "The incidents of victims of lust told in this book are such that if I found a person putting that book indiscriminately before the children I would institute a criminal proceeding against them for doing it."

The school board returned the copy of *Woman, Church and State* to a furious Gage. When asked her opinion of Comstock by a reporter, she pulled no punches:

> *I look upon him as a man who is mentally and morally un-balanced, not knowing right from wrong or the facts of history from "tales of lust." Being intellectually weak, Anthony*

> *Comstock misrepresents all works upon which he presumes to pass judgment, and is as dangerous to liberty of speech and of the press as were the old inquisitors, whom he somewhat resembles. A fool as a press censor is more to be feared than a knave, and Comstock seems to be a union of both fool and knave. Buddha declared the only sin to be ignorance. If this be true, Anthony Comstock is a great sinner.* [82]

Living always by the words she'd spoken to the audience in her first woman's rights speech in 1852, Gage welcomed the attack from her enemies. It let her know she was on the right course: *Fear not any attempt to frown down the revolution already commenced;* she had advised forty-one years before, *nothing is more fertile aid of reform, than any attempt to check it.* She was invigorated, she told the reporter:

> *You wish to know the effect of this Comstock-Catholic attack upon me? It has acted like a tonic. I have not been well through the summer, not having recovered from over-work on* **Woman, Church and State,** *but the moment I learned of Comstock's letter and read the falsities so freely printed in regard to my book, I grew better and feel myself able to meet all enemies of whatever name or nature.*

The Church took up the Comstock cause and the papers reported that Catholics and Protestants alike were calling for the suppression of *Woman, Church and State.* Gage exuberantly wrote her son; *All it now needs is to get into the papal Index Expurgatorious.* [83]

Matilda Joslyn Gage lived with her youngest daughter Maud during the winters she was writing this book. Maud's husband, a creative genius who told wonderful stories but had little practical sense, was devoted to his mother-in-law, in whom he found an intellectual mentor. Matilda told her son-in-law to write down the stories he told his eager sons, and L. Frank Baum had the good sense to listen to his mother-in-law. She seems to have provided him with subject matter for his books, as well. In *Ozma of Oz,* for example, the wicked Nome King, who is the essence of a patriarchal ruler deeply fears just one thing—eggs. Baum may have taken the symbol from *Woman, Church and State,* where Gage writes:

> *Anciently motherhood was represented by a sphere or circle. The circle, like the mundane egg, which is but an elongated circle, contains everything in itself and is the true microcosm. It is eternity, it is feminine, the creative force, representing spirit.*[84]

The church-free, female-led utopia Baum created in his fourteen Oz books somewhat resembles the Matriarchate his mother-in-law details in the first chapter of this book. The trinity of Oz (Glinda, Ozma and Dorothy) protects its peaceful structure, ensuring that all inhabitants are treated respectfully and have what they need. Perhaps the books may be read as a matching set. *Woman, Church and State* is the dystopia, documenting the devastating damage of male rule, while Oz is the utopian vision of the natural, pre-Christian world in which woman's authority prevails.

The Woman's Bible

W HEN WOMAN INTERPRETS the Bible for herself, it will be in the interest of a higher morality, a purer home, Gage predicted in *Woman, Church and State.* It may be impossible to determine whether Stanton or Gage first had the idea of interpreting the Bible. More importantly, it may not matter. The writing of the movement's two principal theoreticians mirrors each other in the 1890s. Both focused on the church's primary role in woman's oppression; both saw this as the most important work of their lives.

Stanton approached Gage about collaborating with her on a book containing women's interpretation of the Bible. Apparently she was past her white-hot anger at Stanton ("quick to anger, quick to forgive," the family describes the Joslyn temper) and was willing to give her another chance, for Gage said yes. The work, for Gage, was always the important thing—more important than interpersonal tensions produced in the process of doing it. She put her pen in motion and created the framework for the book.

The Bible could be understood on many levels, she wrote, as *custodian of the profoundest secrets of the "ancient mysteries," a spiritual book of trebly veiled,* [both interpretations Gage went on to write for the book] *or as the physical and religious history of the world in its most material forms.* General interpretations, however, were not the point. *Our present quest is not what the mystic or the spiritual character of the Bible may be; we are investigating its influence upon woman under Judaism and Christianity, and pronounce it evil.*[85]

While it looked like the two best minds of the movement were once again working together and would collaborate on what might be the greatest work either one of them had accomplished, that feminist masterpiece would never happen. While Gage understood they were to be partners in this production, once again Stanton had lightly made a commitment that she moved away from without telling Gage.

Please at once let me know the reason that the copyright of **The Woman's Bible** *was not taken out in my name as well as your own,* Gage challenged Stanton. *You wrote me to so take it out then said you would have Mrs. Colby—who was in Washington—do the work.* Colby had copyrighted the work in Stanton's name alone, and had written Gage "that she had 'no instruction' and 'no reason' for incorporating any name" with Stanton's. With typical straightforwardness, Gage asked Stanton to explain: *Please at once let me know what this omission of my name means. If it was a mistake, perhaps it can be changed even yet, as you will not get the copyright papers in some months.*[86]

Gage gave Stanton detailed instructions on how to make the change, but apparently it was no mistake. Stanton had simply decided to edit the book on her own and failed to inform Gage of her decision.

There is an absence in *The Woman's Bible* that becomes apparent when you compare it with *Woman, Church and State.* Gage analyzed the church's complicity in the sexual violation of women and children without censoring or hesitation. She wrote boldly about sexual issues and identified the foundation of abuse in Christianity. The practice of sexual abuse by priests, the realities of child prostitutes and sexual slavery she places at the door of the church. Gage paved the way, why didn't Stanton follow it? The absence of examination of sexual references in *The Woman's Bible* is hard to explain. "It was just not done at the time" doesn't hold water, because Freethinkers were being jailed under the Comstock laws for challenging each roadblock in the way of a woman's right to control her own body, from birth control to marital rape, in the 1890s.

It's something to contemplate what these two great minds might have accomplished had they collaborated in an interpretation of the Bible at this advanced and wise stage of their lives. The unflinching courage of Gage would have been matched with Stanton's bold and clear wit. Gage would have firmed-up Stanton's backbone, and the unevenness of *The Woman's Bible*, resulting from the gamut of the contributor's ideologies, would have instead carried Gage's laser-focus trademark. Far the superior writer, Stanton would have cleaned up Gage's sentences and honed her brilliance into a comprehensible form. The loss to the woman's movement of this analysis of religion that never happened is inestimable.

Gage's health declined. She nearly died in 1896, and never completely recovered her vigor. While continuing to write, she published little of it. Anthony visited her in Chicago during the fall of 1897, and the two women may have found some resolution. Shortly after, Gage became ill and never again left the house. She rallied briefly, and planned to attend the 50th anniversary celebration of the first woman's rights convention in February 1898, but wasn't able to make it. She wrote an address, "Woman's Demand for Freedom; Its Influence Upon the World," which Mary Seymour Howell read at the NAWSA convention. "Mrs. Gage was for so long active as an officer of the NAWSA that for her as for Mrs. Stanton, an exception was made to the general rule against papers not presented by the author" the convention report explained. On March 13, she suffered a stroke, which completely paralyzed her. Gage died five days later, never having recovered consciousness. "The end," her daughter Helen said, "was very quiet and peaceful, just a gradual shortening of the breath."

Victoria Woodhull (Martin)'s *Humanitarian* in London published one of nearly 100 obituaries that appeared in a variety of publications:

"After death, Mrs. Gage was robed in the dress she liked best, and placed on a couch in her room. There she lay calm and peaceful as if asleep and her children, all of whom were there, spent hours sitting near, while the grandchildren went in and out as they chose without any of that fear and dread which oftentimes accompanies the presence of death. No crepe was on the door, just a large bouquet of white and lavender hyacinths, tied with lavender ribbon."[87]

At her own request, Gage was cremated. Her daughter Maud took her mother's ashes back to Fayetteville for burial in the summer.

Gage's nemesis, Frances Willard—the woman who pronounced that "the sweetest words are mother, home and heaven"—died in February. Gage had the last word. Carved on her tombstone in the Fayetteville cemetery for eternity is her motto: *There is a word sweeter than mother, home or heaven. That word is Liberty.*

Written Out of History

G AGE NEVER BELIEVED that this was the end, as she had explained to her grandson, Harry Carpenter, the year before her death:

There is one thing I want you to remember first of all: what is called 'death' by people is not death. You are more alive than ever

you were after what is called death. Death is only a journey, like
going to another country. You are alive when you travel to
Aberdeen just as much as when you stay in Edgeley and it is the
same with what is called death. After people have been gone
for awhile they come back and live in another body, in another
family and have another name. Sometimes they live in another
country and nation.[88]

Oh, she'd be back, all right. Her belief in that was "unshakable,"
according to her children. There was something else. The work.
It had all been done for those who would come after, for the
"Daughters of 1976," as Gage had dedicated the *Declaration of Rights
of Women* in 1876. Her final editorial in the *National Citizen and Ballot
Box* carried her belief in the future:

To those who fancy we are near the end of the battle or that the
reformer's path is strewn with roses, we may say then nay. The
thick of the fight has just begun; the hottest part of the warfare
is yet to come, and those who enter it must be willing to give up
father, mother and comforts for its sake. Neither shall we who
carry on the fight, reap the great reward. We are battling for the
good of those who shall come after us; they, not ourselves,
shall enter into the harvest.[89]

You live on in your work, Gage believed.

At first that seemed true. Tributes came in from around the
country. Stanton eulogized: "the Woman's Suffrage Association has
lost one of its most able speakers, writers and actual thinkers."
The Chicago Political Equality League resolved: "that Mrs. Gage's
devotion to principle and straightforward and fearless advocacy of
what she considered right, regardless of applause or opposition, merit
and receive our admiration." Catherine Devereux Blake, the daughter
of one of her long-time coworkers, later recalled, "I always loved and
admired her greatly." Placing her alongside Susan B. Anthony,
Elizabeth Cady Stanton and Isabella Beecher Hooker, Blake concluded, "I think that in some ways she was the greatest of those four
women."[90] Honoring Gage's "deep and lasting mark" on the

movement during the Memorial tributes at the NAWSA convention the following year, Antoinette Brown Blackwell recalled her first speech at the 1852 Syracuse convention, and how Wendell Phillips said of her then, "She came to us an unknown woman. She leaves us a co-worker whose reputation is established."[91]

The *New Era* had predicted in December 1885 that "When final and complete victory shall shed its illuminating light upon historic annals of the great, moral and political reform known as the Woman Suffrage Movement, more and more will the name and services of Matilda Joslyn Gage be recognized and appreciated."

The opposite would be the case.

Anthony lived longer than either Stanton or Gage. President of the NAWSA from 1892 to 1900, she made her name so inextricably tied to the movement that her telling of its history became the accepted version. Anthony chose the biographer she wanted to write the story of her life and the movement and sat beside Ida Husted Harper as the young journalist carried out her bidding. By the time Harper completed their fourth volume of the *History of Woman Suffrage*, she and Anthony had removed Gage's most important work from history.

They began in the Preface, where they denied Gage's work as co-author with Stanton of the first three volumes, reducing her to a helpful assistant. They sanitized the merger between the American and National associations, making no mention of dissenters. The union was described in one paragraph and treated as an inevitable occurrence. The Woman's National Liberal Union was not mentioned in Harper's painstakingly detailed list of women's organizations, while groups like the National Floral Emblem Society, which was created to choose a national and state flower, were considered important enough to mention. Harper did not even acknowledge Gage's last address in her detailed account of the 1898 NAWSA convention, although the printed convention report did.

Harper and Anthony wrote the history and then destroyed the evidence. When Anthony's biography and the fourth volume of the *History* were completed, Anthony and Harper arranged for the burning of all of Anthony's letters, an undertaking that took

Anthony's sister a month to carry out. None of the dissenters to the union published their side, and Anthony's version stood, unchallenged, as the historically accurate account.[92]

"Fanatical and solemn without impressiveness; an uncompromising and unpersuasive attack on church and state—especially church—for their attitude towards woman." This is the way *Woman, Church and State* was described in a 1913 bibliography put together by the National American Woman Suffrage Association.[93] The woman's movement had become religiously respectable (Stanton's *The Woman's Bible,* from which the organization had earlier disassociated itself, is not even mentioned on the list) and the process of writing the far more radical suffragist Matilda Joslyn Gage out of history was virtually complete. While the conservative movement may have silenced her voice, the enemy still remembered.

"Christianity and Suffrage have often been at War" headlined a newspaper article by Milwaukee Archbishop Messmer in 1913. "Of the great triumvirate of the American suffrage cause, Elizabeth Cady Stanton, Susan B. Anthony and Matilda Joslyn Gage, joint authors of the *History of Woman Suffrage* and leaders in the organized movement," Messmer wrote, "all were unorthodox in religious matters." His strongest attack, not surprisingly, he reserved for Gage who, he wrote, "in her last work, *Woman, Church and State* declared that 'the church has enslaved woman,' and sought to show of how little value Christianity has been & is to civilization etc., etc."

Messmer contended, "God has determined that woman should be inferior to man…There is far too much un-Christian infidel sentiment connected with the Woman suffrage movement."[94] While Gage would have welcomed the battle, that charge by Messmer was precisely what the NAWSA feared. The last thing they wanted to do was to ruffle the clergy's feathers. It was far easier and more expedient to simply rid the movement's history of its troublesome and irritatingly radical foremothers. Matilda Joslyn Gage—the most outspoken, the least compromising, the woman with the most far-reaching analysis of woman's oppression—was the most obvious target.

The erasure, of course, could not be permanent. Needing a connection with a past that saw beyond the vote, the current wave of feminism "discovered" Matilda Joslyn Gage. The words of the Chicago Suffrage League at Gage's death now stand as a prediction of the effect she continues to have 100 years after her death:

> "Her success in rousing other women to action was marked, and she always reminded the writer of some invincible hero battling for a just cause, that no evil could daunt and for whom the word fear had no meaning. Her keen sense of injustice has caused her to set lance in rest for every wronged woman...Many a young soul has been stirred from its drowsy sleep of ignorant ease by its bugle note, and interested in the great struggle for freedom."[95]

Despite all she endured, Gage maintained her belief that human beings could create the ability to behave well. Having been "born with a hatred of oppression," as she often said, she had a corresponding deep-seated love of liberty. It was to that vision she dedicated her life, to the ongoing fight for liberty—political, social, religious and economic—for all people. Freedom, she believed, was an achievable goal:

> *The world is now full of subjects to compel great thoughts. Woman's experiences broaden, deepen, embolden her. She sees life as never before, as never before she dares to be herself. The progress of life is a growth headword; as the spirit brain increases, morality increases and humanity becomes more free. True civilization is a recognition of the rights of others at every point of contact, and when this takes place the world will step out of the darkness of heathendom into a full light of a religious and political civilization grander than any of which it has yet dreamed.*[96]

Notes

1. *Report of the International Council of Women, assembled by the National Woman Suffrage Association*, Washington, D.C., March 25 to April 1, 1888. (Washington, D. C.: National Woman Suffrage Association, 1888), 347.

2. *Speech of Mrs. M.E.J. Gage at the Woman's Rights Convention held at Syracuse, New York, September 1852.* Woman's Right Tract No. 7. (Syracuse: Master's Print, 1852); *New York Tribune*, 14 September 1852.

3. Matilda Joslyn Gage to Lillie Devereux Blake, 2 May 1890, Blake Papers, Missouri Historical Society.

4. *Speech of Mrs. M.E.J. Gage at the Woman's Rights Convention held at Syracuse, New York, September 1852; New York Tribune*, September 14, 1852.

5. *Report of the International Council of Women*, 347.

6. They shall not make baldness upon their head; neither shall they shave off the corner of their beard, nor make any cuttings in their flesh.

7. The Gage-Sunderland debates carried in (Syracuse) *Star*, October 1852; also *History of Woman Suffrage* I: 43-45. Arno Press and the *New York Times* reprinted all six volumes of the *History* (New York: 1969).

8. *Report of the International Council of Women*, 347.

9. "Flag Presentation to the Third Onondaga Regiment," (Syracuse) *Onondaga Standard*, 3 September 1862.

10. *History Of Woman Suffrage* II: 89.

11. "Woman's Rights Catechism," (Fayetteville NY) *Weekly Recorder*, 27 July 1871.

12. Katherine Devereux Blake and Margaret Louise Wallace, *Champion of Women* (New York: Fleming H. Revell Company, 1943), 168.

13. *The United States on Trial; not Susan B. Anthony. An Account of the Proceedings on the Trial of Susan B. Anthony, on the Charge of Illegal Voting, at the Presidential Election in November 1872.* 1874. (Reprint ed. New York: Arno Press, 1974), 179-205.

14. *Minor v. Happersett*, 53 Mo., 58, and 21 Wallace, 162, 1874; *History of Woman Suffrage* II: Chapter XXV, "Trials and Decisions," 586-755.

15. *History of Woman Suffrage* II: 689, 749.

16. *History of Woman Suffrage* III: 59-60; "Woman Suffrage," [1877] newspaper clipping, scrapbook, Gage family private collection; "Appeal to Women Citizens of the United States," *National Citizen Extra*, Fall 1878.

17. Manuscript of Matilda Joslyn Gage, Susan B. Anthony scrapbook 6, Rare Books, Library of Congress. I am grateful to Pat Holland of the Stanton-Anthony Papers project at Amherst for making me aware of this manuscript.

18. *Syracuse Journal*, 7 May 1871.

19. "Women Tax Payers," (Fayetteville, N.Y.) *Weekly Recorder,* [1873], scrapbook of writings, Gage Papers, Schlesinger Library; "Tea and Taxes," *Chicago Tribune,* [1873] and "Call for December 16, 1873 Mass Meeting," Gage scrapbook, Library of Congress.

20. Matilda Joslyn Gage to Laura DeForce Gordon, 23 April 1876, Gordon Papers, Bancroft Library.

21. *History of Woman Suffrage* III: 34. Chapter XXVII, "The Centennial Year," (1-56) has a complete and vivid description of events during the year. Also see Sally Roesch Wagner, *A Time of Protest, Suffragists Challenge the Republic: 1870-1887.* (Aberdeen, S.D.: Sky Carrier Press, 1998), Chapter 6.

22. Matilda Joslyn Gage to Laura DeForce Gordon, 31 July 1876, Gordon Papers, Bancroft Library.

23. Susan B. Anthony to Martha Coffin Wright, 1 January 1873, Garrison Papers, Smith College.

24. *National Citizen and Ballot Box* Extra, Fall 1878; Matilda Joslyn Gage to Laura DeForce Gordon, 31 July 1876, Gordon Papers, Bancroft Library.

25. Matilda Joslyn Gage to Harriet Robinson, 28 February 1879, Robinson Papers, Schlesinger Library; Matilda Joslyn Gage to Laura DeForce Gordon, 29 December 1880, Gordon Papers, Bancroft Library.

26. "History of Woman Suffrage Agreement," 15 November 1876, Harper Papers, Huntington Library.

27. Robinson-Gage correspondence, April and May 1879, Robinson Papers, Schlesinger Library; Theodore Stanton and Harriet Stanton Blatch, Eds., *Elizabeth Cady Stanton as Revealed in her Letters, Diary and Reminiscences,* Vol. II. (N.Y.: Harper and Brothers, 1922), 226; Susan B. Anthony to Olympia Brown, 26 February 1881, Brown Papers, Schlesinger Library.

28. Susan B. Anthony to Elizabeth Boynton Harbert, 22 June 1885, Harbert Papers, Huntington Library; Matilda Joslyn Gage letters to Thomas Clarkson Gage, 1883-1885, Gage Papers, Schlesinger Library.

29. Matilda Joslyn Gage to Laura De Force Gordon, 29 December 1880, Gordon Papers, Bancroft Library; Matilda Joslyn Gage to Lillie Devereux Blake, 21 April 1888, Blake Papers, Smith College Library.

30. Susan B. Anthony to Elizabeth Boynton Harbert, 28 September 1885, Harbert Papers, Huntington Library; Ida Husted Harper, *The Life and Work of Susan B. Anthony,* Vol. 1. (Indianapolis: Bowen-Merrill Co. 1899), 25. Correspondence of the women (1876-1886) indicates what work and writing each woman was doing on the *History.*

31. Ida Husted Harper, *The Life and Work of Susan B. Anthony.* Three volumes. (Indianapolis: Bowen-Merrill Co. 1899); *History of Woman Suffrage* I: 8; Elizabeth Cady Stanton and Revising Committee, *The Woman's Bible.* (New York: European Publishing Company; 1898).

32. *History of Woman Suffrage* IV: V, 164, 1070; Katherine Anthony, *Susan B. Anthony, Her Personal History and Her Era.* (Garden City, New York: Doubleday and Company, 1954). Pages 474-475 reveal the letter burning.

33. In private family collection.

34. *History of Woman Suffrage* III: 60; (Toledo, Ohio) Ballot Box, April 1878.

35. 1880 Suffrage Campaign in *National Citizen and Ballot Box* Editorial, October 1879; (Fayetteville) *Weekly Recorder*, 28 October 1880; *Syracuse Journal*, 14 and 16 October 1880.

36. "The Woman Suffrage Question," *Syracuse Journal,* [January 1872], Gage scrapbook, Library of Congress.

37. 1884 Equal Rights Party election ticket, Gage Papers, Schlesinger Library.

38. *New York Evening Telegram,* 24 March 1886; Mary Seymour Howell to Lillie Devereux Blake, 31 March 1886, Blake Papers, Missouri Historical Society; "Women Express Their Preferences," *New York Tribune,* 28 October 1886.

39. Susan B. Anthony, Matilda Joslyn Gage, Rachel G. Foster, Mary Wright Sewall and Lilly Devereux Blake, "Protest Against the Unjust Interpretation of the Constitution Presented on Behalf of the Women of the United States by Officers of the National Woman Suffrage Association, 17 September 1887", Blake Papers, Missouri Historical Society.

40. Matilda Joslyn Gage to Caroline Alden Huling, 9 June 1888, Huling Papers, University of Illinois at Chicago.

41. Matilda Joslyn Gage, "Woman as Inventor." Woman Suffrage Tract, No. 1. (Fayetteville, New York: F. A. Darling, Printer, 1870).

42. Matilda Joslyn Gage, "Who Planned the Tennessee Campaign of 1862?" National Citizen Tract No. 1, (N.P 1880).

43. *National Citizen and Ballot Box,* April 1878.

44. *National Citizen and Ballot Box,* May-July, 1878.

45. Gage's writing on the Haudenosaunee and her adoption into the Wolf Clan of the Mohawk Nation is covered in Sally Roesch Wagner, *The Untold Story of the Iroquois Influence on Early Feminists* (Aberdeen, S.D.: Sky Carrier Press, 1996).

46. Matilda Joslyn Gage, "Indian Citizenship," *National Citizen and Ballot Box,* May 1878.

47. Matilda Joslyn Gage to Thomas Clarkson Gage, "Dear Clarkey," 1876, Gage Papers, Schlesinger Library.

48. "The Watkins Convention," 212-213, Gage scrapbook, Library of Congress.

49. *Woman, Church and State*, Chapter nine.

50. *National Citizen and Ballot Box,* August/September 1878.

51. *National Citizen and Ballot Box,* April and May 1879.

52. *Proceedings of the International Council of Women,* 1888, 400-407.

53. Matilda Joslyn Gage to Thomas Clarkson Gage & Helen Leslie Gage, 8 April 1888 [Misdated, is March] and Matilda Joslyn Gage to Thomas Clarkson Gage, 26 May 1888, Gage Papers, Schlesinger Library.

54. Matilda Joslyn Gage to Elizabeth Cady Stanton, 13 July 1888.

55. Anna Gordon, *The Beautiful Life of Frances Willard.* (Chicago: Woman's Temperance Publishing Association, 1898), 114-115.

56. Matilda Joslyn Gage to Elizabeth Cady Stanton, 13 July 1888; Alma Lutz, *Created Equal* (New York: John Day Company, 1940), 276.

57. WCTU and Prohibition Party information in *Woman's Tribune* throughout the Fall, 1888.

58. Matilda Joslyn Gage to Thomas Clarkson Gage, 26 May 1888, Gage Papers, Schlesinger Library.

59. Matilda Joslyn Gage to Caroline Alden Huling, 9 June 1888, Huling Papers, University of Illinois at Chicago.

60. Matilda Joslyn Gage to Harriet Robinson, 11 March 1890, Robinson Papers, Schlesinger Library.

61. Rachel Foster, "Negotiations between the American and National Woman Suffrage Associations," Vassar College Library; Scrapbook of clippings on union negotiations in Robinson Papers, Schlesinger Library.

62. Harriet Robinson and Harriette Shattuck's notes on union, Gage letters to them, and scrapbook of union clippings in Robinson Papers, Schlesinger Library; (Washington) *Evening Star,* 21-25 January 1889; (Washington) *Post,* 22 and 23 January 1889.

63. Matilda Joslyn Gage, "A Statement of Facts, Private. To members of the NWSA only." Gage and Brown Papers, Schlesinger Library; Matilda Joslyn Gage to Harriet Robinson and Harriette Shattuck, February to December 1889 and January to March 1890, Robinson Papers, Schlesinger Library; Matilda Joslyn Gage to Elizabeth Boynton Harbert, 26 March 1889, Harbert Papers, Huntington Library.

64. Susan B. Anthony to Olympia Brown, 11 March 1889, Brown Papers, Schlesinger Library.

65. Elizabeth Cady Stanton to Olympia Brown, 8 May 1888, Brown Papers, Schlesinger Library.

66. Susan B. Anthony to Eliza Wright Osbourne, 5 February and 5 March 1890, Garrison Papers, Sophia Smith Library, Smith College; Susan B. Anthony to Lillie Devereux Blake, 6 February 1890, Blake Papers, Missouri Historical Society.

67. Elizabeth Cady Stanton to Matilda Joslyn Gage, 19 October 1889, printed in *Liberal Thinker,* January 1890.

68. Stanton interview in (Washington) *Post,* 9 February 1890.

69. Blake and Wallace, *Champion of Women,* 115.

70. Anthony to Eliza Wright Osbourne, 5 February and 5 March 1890, Garrison Papers, Sophia Smith Library, Smith College; Anthony to Blake, 6 February 1890, Blake Papers, Missouri Historical Society.

71. Matilda Joslyn Gage to Thomas Clarkson Gage, 7 March 1890, Gage Papers, Schlesinger Library.

72. Ibid.

73. WNLU Convention in (Washington) *Post, Star* and *Critic,* 22-26 February 1890.

74. Matilda Joslyn Gage to Thomas Clarkson Gage, 7 March 1890, Gage Papers, Schlesinger Library.

75. *Woman, Church And State*, Chapter nine, footnote 10.

76. Parker Pillsbury to Lillie Devereux Blake, 11 April 1890, Missouri Historical Society.

77. Matilda Joslyn Gage to Thomas Clarkson Gage, 13 August 1890, Gage Papers, Schlesinger Library.

78. Matilda Joslyn Gage to Thomas Clarkson Gage, 7 March 1890, Gage Papers, Schlesinger Library.

79. Promotional material in original edition of *Woman, Church And State*, (Chicago: Charles Kerr, 1893).

80. *Truth Seeker*, 1 July 1893.

81. Matilda Joslyn Gage to Thomas Clarkson Gage, 11 July 1893, Gage Papers, Schlesinger Library.

82. (Fayetteville) *Recorder* and (Syracuse) *Onondoga Standard*, 16-23 August 1894.

83. Matilda Joslyn Gage to Thomas Clarkson Gage, 3 And 6 August 1894, Matilda Gage Papers.

84. *Woman, Church and State*, Chapter 1.

85. *The Woman's Bible*, 176-209.

86. Matilda Joslyn Gage to Elizabeth Cady Stanton, 28 May 1895, Colby Papers, Archives Division Wisconsin Historical Society.

87. (London) *Humanitarian*, June 1898, 423-424.

88. Matilda Joslyn Gage to Harry Carpenter, 21 January 1897, Jocelyn Burdick Collection.

89. *National Citizen and Ballot Box*, October 1881.

90. Blake and Wallace, *Champion of Women*, 115.

91. *History of Woman Suffrage* IV: 345.

92. *History of Woman Suffrage* IV: V, 164, 1070; Katherine Anthony, *Susan B. Anthony, Her Personal History And Her Era*, (Garden City, New York: Doubleday and Company, 1954) 474-475 reveals the letter burning.

93. Margarer Ladd Franklin, *The Case For Woman Suffrage: A Bibliography*. (New York: National College Equal Suffrage League. Sold by the National American Woman Suffrage Association, 1913), 67.

94. Helen Leslie Gage writing, Betty Baum Papers.

95. Maud Gage Baum scrapbook of Matilda Joslyn Gage obituaries, Gage papers, Schlesinger Library.

96. "The Foundation of Sovereignty," *Woman's Tribune*, April 1887.

Matilda Joslyn Gage at age 62 (February 1888)
Photograph by son-in-law L. Frank Baum

Additional Matilda Joslyn Gage materials (poster, button, notecard and postcard) available from:

Syracuse Cultural Workers
(315) 474-1132
www.nonviolence.org.

Other books by Sally Roesch Wagner available from Sky Carrier Press:

Daughters of Dakota (six volume series)

The Untold Story of the Iroquois Influence on Early Feminists

Elizabeth Cady Stanton Thunders from the Pulpit

A Time of Protest—Suffragists Challenge the Republic: 1870-1887

Celebrating Your Cultural Heritage by Telling the Untold Stories

About the Author

One of the first women to receive a doctorate in this country for work in women's studies, (UC Santa Cruz), Sally Roesch Wagner was a founder of one of the first college-level women's studies programs (CSU Sacramento). Having taught women's studies for twenty years, Dr. Wagner now tours the country as a writer, lecturer and historical performer, "bringing to life" Matilda Joslyn Gage and Elizabeth Cady Stanton.

One of the scholars interviewed in Ken Burns's upcoming production about Susan B. Anthony and Elizabeth Cady Stanton, Wagner also served as an historian in the PBS special, "One Woman, One Vote," and has been interviewed several times on National Public Radio's *All Things Considered.* She was the Jeanette K. Watson Women's Studies Distinguished Visiting Professor in the Humanities at Syracuse University in Spring 1997, and has been a consultant to the Woman's Rights National Historical Park and the National Women's History Project.

During the summer of 1998, Wagner curated an exhibit, "She Who Holds the Sky: Matilda Joslyn Gage, Mother, Radical, Scholar," for the Women's Rights National Historical Park in Seneca Falls, New York. She also developed a curriculum and curated a traveling exhibit (sponsored by the Elizabeth Cady Stanton Foundation) documenting the influence of Iroquois women on early women's rights activists Lucretia Mott, Elizabeth Cady Stanton and Matilda Joslyn Gage. Wagner keynoted the opening session of the 1998 National Women's Studies Association convention with a lecture on this topic.

Her essays have appeared in *The Encyclopedia of Women and World Religion* (forthcoming); *Women Public Speakers in the United States, 1800-1925,* (1993); *Indian Roots of American Democracy* (1992); *Iroquois Women: an Anthology* (1990); and *Handbook of American Women's History* (1990). She has published articles in *On the Issues, Northeast Indian Quarterly, Indian Country Today, Hartford Courant, Women's History Network News* and the *Sacramento Bee.*